FILLING THE LEADERSHIP PIPELINE

FILLING THE LEADERSHIP PIPELINE

Edited by
Robert B. Kaiser

Center for Creative Leadership
Greensboro, North Carolina

The Center for Creative Leadership is an international, nonprofit educational institution founded in 1970 to advance the understanding, practice, and development of leadership for the benefit of society worldwide. As a part of this mission, it publishes books and reports that aim to contribute to a general process of inquiry and understanding in which ideas related to leadership are raised, exchanged, and evaluated. The ideas presented in its publications are those of the author or authors.

The Center thanks you for supporting its work through the purchase of this volume. If you have comments, suggestions, or questions about any CCL Press publication, please contact the Director of Publications at the address given below.

Center for Creative Leadership
Post Office Box 26300
Greensboro, North Carolina 27438-6300
336-288-7210 • www.ccl.org

Center for
Creative
Leadership

NORTH AMERICA EUROPE ASIA
www.ccl.org

CCL No. 354

Library of Congress Cataloging-in-Publication Data

Filling the leadership pipeline / edited by Robert B. Kaiser
      p. cm.
   ISBN 1-882197-90-9 [ISBN-13: 978-1-882197-90-3]
  1. Leadership. 2. Management. I. Kaiser, Robert B. II. Title.

   HD57.7.F54 2005
   658.4'092—dc22

2005028310

Table of Contents

Acknowledgments

It is a privilege to work with and learn from skilled colleagues. And it is the proverbial icing on the cake when they are as rewarding personally as they are competent professionally. Such was the case for the project that began as a panel presentation at the nineteenth annual conference for the Society for Industrial and Organizational Psychology and resulted in this volume. For their pearls of wisdom, steadfast work habits, and openness to (my sometimes heavy-handed) editorial suggestions, I am grateful to Pat Weik, Arthur Freedman, Amy Kates, Skip Leonard, and Jennifer Martineau and her colleagues, Greg Laskow, Lisa Moye, and Dick Phillips. Thank you for making this volume possible.

I also appreciate the encouragement and support for this project received unfailingly from David DeVries and Bob Kaplan.

Dedication

This volume is dedicated to the life and career of Diane Downey. I met Diane for the first time when we were both presenting in a workshop on executive talent management sponsored by the Human Resources Planning Society. She struck me immediately as very sharp, no-nonsense, gutsy, and utterly down-to-earth. She proved herself to be every bit of those qualities and more.

As we got to know each other and I explored her work on leadership and organizational design, it became evident that Diane's savvy and insight were born of firsthand experience forged by deep reflection. She had the mental agility of a first-rate scholar with all of the practicality of a seasoned executive. It turned out that she came by this rare combination honestly: prior to building her own internationally recognized consulting firm, Downey Kates Associates, she held senior corporate positions responsible for management and organization development at Citibank USA and Harper & Row Publishing. Diane also held faculty appointments at the University of Maryland, Howard University, and Antioch College, and taught courses at Cornell and New York University. What made her intellect and street smarts all the more palpable, however, was her deep compassion. As well as a successful businesswoman, Diane was a skilled therapist, social activist, generous colleague, caring teacher, and, most of all, a dear friend.

For all of these reasons, this volume is dedicated to Diane Downey. I think she would be proud to be part of an interdisciplinary, multicollaborator effort to help organizations and the individuals that populate them make their full contribution and find deep fulfillment. After all, this was an enduring theme across her many professional and personal activities.

Greensboro, North Carolina   Robert B. Kaiser
May 2005

The Authors

Diane Downey was president and founder of Downey Kates Associates and worked extensively in the area of new leader assimilation. Her book *Assimilating New Leaders: The Key to Executive Retention* (AMACOM, 2001) won the 2002 Book of the Year award from the Society for Human Resource Management. Diane earned a master's degree in counseling psychology from the University of Iowa and completed her doctoral coursework at New York University.

Arthur M. Freedman is a consulting psychologist who specializes in organization development and change. He is the director of the master of science degree in organization development offered by American University and the NTL Institute. He has been a member of the NTL Institute since 1969. He is a fellow and former board member of the Society of Consulting Psychology and past president of the Society of Psychologists in Management.

Arthur earned both his B.S. and M.B.A. at Boston University's College of Business Administration and his Ph.D. in personality and clinical psychology at the University of Chicago. He is CEO of Quantum Associates and has consulted throughout North America and in Sweden, Russia, Western Europe, the United Kingdom, Singapore, and Zimbabwe. He has published widely on management development, OD, and consultation. His most recent book, with R. E. "Zack" Zackrison, is *Finding Your Way in the Consulting Jungle* (Jossey-Bass, 2001).

Amy Kates is a principal partner of Downey Kates Associates in New York. Her work focuses on organization design, particularly the challenges that confront complex, global organizations. She also consults in the areas of executive team development, talent assessment, and HR strategy. Amy works with leaders and their teams to assess organizational issues, reshape structures and processes, and build depth of management capability. She is a skilled diagnostician and designer, and helps her clients to understand organizational issues, the options, and their implications, and to make good decisions. She is an author, with Jay Galbraith and Diane Downey, of *Designing Dynamic Organizations: A Hands-on Guide for Leaders at All Levels* (AMACOM, 2001).

In addition to her consulting work, she teaches organization design in the Executive M.B.A. program at the University of Denmark. She is also on the Board of Directors of the Organization Design Forum. Amy holds a master's degree in city and regional planning from Cornell University.

Greg Laskow is the Custom Solutions manager with the Center for Creative Leadership's European branch, located in Brussels, Belgium. Headquartered in Greensboro, North Carolina, CCL is an international, nonprofit educational institution devoted to research and teaching on leadership in the private and public sectors. It is one of the largest institutions in the world focusing on leadership.

As a key player on the Custom Solutions design team, Greg provides considerable experience and expertise in creating unique client-specific programs. In addition to his custom work, he trains in The Looking Glass Experience program and the Center's flagship open-enrollment offering, the Leadership Development Program (LDP)®. Greg has collaboratively codesigned custom programs for leadership development across a variety of public and private sectors, some of which include financial, manufacturing, service, health care, telecommunications, transportation, consumer, and government industries. He is particularly sensitive to and passionate about the various global and cultural differences that must be considered in a developmental process for leaders and organizations.

Greg joined the Center from Farr Associates, Inc., where he served as vice president of the personal executive development line of business. Prior to his current role, Greg served as a senior program associate at CCL's Greensboro campus.

He received his bachelor's and master's degrees from the University of Scranton and a Ph.D. in counseling psychology from Texas Tech University. In 1994, Greg retired from the U.S. Army with the rank of colonel.

H. Skipton Leonard is vice president and executive consultant at Personnel Decisions International's Washington, DC, office. Prior to his current positions, Skip served as head of the executive coaching and assessment practices as well as general manager in PDI's Washington office. He has more than twenty-five years' experience helping organizations hire, retain, and develop the best executive and managerial talent. He is especially interested in helping organizations develop executive and management leadership and talent, build high-performing leadership teams, and behave more adaptively, creatively, and strategically in rapidly changing market conditions. He is a frequent presenter at national conferences on leadership and leadership development, has numerous publications to his credit, and has coauthored a graduate-level management textbook.

Skip is the founding editor of *Consulting Psychology Journal,* a past president of the American Psychological Association's Society of Consulting

Psychology, and an APA fellow. He received his doctoral degree in psychology from New York University.

Jennifer Martineau serves as the director of the Center for Creative Leadership's Design and Evaluation Center. Jennifer earned a Ph.D. in industrial and organizational psychology from the Pennsylvania State University. At CCL since 1993 and with over fifteen years' experience in the field of evaluation, she has focused her attention on the evaluation of leadership development initiatives. She is recognized as contributing significantly to the growth and improvement of CCL's evaluation practice as a whole, as well as developing numerous evaluation tools and processes. Jennifer serves as internal evaluation coach to CCL faculty and staff, CCL clients, and other leadership development professionals.

Jennifer approaches the evaluation of leadership development initiatives from the perspective that evaluation needs should drive the design of these initiatives and should therefore be considered a part of these initiatives from their inception. In this framework, evaluation helps to shape initiatives in a way that is more certain to *create* desired impact.

During her time at CCL, Jennifer has worked with a wide array of client organizations, including international for-profit and not-for-profit organizations, school systems, and government agencies. Her work can be found in books, peer-reviewed journals, and practitioner-oriented publications. She is a regular presenter at international professional conferences such as the American Evaluation Association, the American Society for Training and Development, and the Society for Industrial and Organizational Psychology, and is a member of these organizations.

Lisa Moye is a senior associate at the Center for Creative Leadership in Greensboro, North Carolina. She is responsible for bringing together CCL client teams focused on developing and managing relationships for clients with complex, long-term needs around customized leadership development initiatives. Additionally, Lisa facilitates the Leadership Development Impact process for client organizations wishing to explore leadership needs at an organizational level. She joined the Center in October 1998.

Prior to her arrival at CCL, Lisa worked for fifteen years as an account manager, primarily in media and contract furniture and design. In this work, she acquired, developed, and managed a wide variety of key client accounts.

Lisa received a degree in industrial and organizational psychology from the University of North Carolina at Greensboro. When not at work, she can often be found enjoying time with family and friends and serving as a volunteer in her community.

Dick Phillips is a senior Intelligence Educator in the Leadership Academy at CIA University. His primary focus is on middle managers in the organization. In this capacity he was one of the designers of the CIA's Managing and Leading Change from the Middle program, which won a best-practices citation from ASTD in 2005. In addition to his activities in the CIA, he works with the other organizations in the U.S. Intelligence Community. He also works with Tigrett Corporation, a company specializing in using historical case studies to teach managers and leaders. Dick has a B.A. in history from Alma College and a Ph.D. in history from the University of Virginia.

Patricia M. Weik has been a consultant with RHR International since 1997 and the director of research and development since September 2000. As head of R&D, she has taken the lead in investigating best practices in the identification and development of future leaders. Her research in this area has resulted in development programs that are closely tied to the company's growth strategy and that focus on the execution of customized development plans for future leaders. The programs have also clarified the roles of senior executives of the companies and the bosses of future leaders in delivering on development goals.

Pat has published work on the topics of future-leader development and the use of culture assessments to accelerate the integration of acquisitions. She continues to consult with select companies in the areas of CEO succession; senior executive development; the design of large-scale, global future-leader development programs; and merger integration.

Prior to joining RHR International, Pat practiced as a clinical geropsychologist at Harvard University, the Veterans Administration, and the St. Louis Behavioral Medicine Institute. Before becoming a licensed psychologist, she was a corporate attorney and an assistant professor of law at St. Louis University Law School. In her legal practice, she specialized in the areas of employment and environmental law. She is a former chair of the Missouri Bar Environmental Law Section, where she led the effort to improve the process of conducting environmental audits during due diligence.

Pat received her law degree from the University of Chicago. She received her Ph.D. in clinical psychology from Northwestern University.

Introduction

Robert B. Kaiser
Kaplan DeVries Inc.

The task at the top of the human resources/organizational development and effectiveness (HR/OD&E) short list these days is ensuring a deep supply of leadership talent that is ready to step into more senior roles when called upon. There are lots of reasons why. Chief among them is that competition is fiercer today than ever before and effective leadership represents a rare source of competitive advantage. With strong leadership and a richly stocked pool of future leaders, organizations prosper and endure.

But the flow in the leadership pipeline has slowed to a trickle. The mass exodus of middle managers initiated in the 1980s by downsizing means that now there are fewer seasoned veterans available for top jobs. Most organization charts and succession maps are noteworthy for the number of blank slots five years out. And the graying and impending retirement of baby boomers coupled with steep and steady declines in skilled entrants to the workforce adds up to an even greater shortage of talent in the U.S. labor market of the early twenty-first century. This could make the "War for Talent" of the late 1990s look more like a street fight.

The Business Case

There is an easy case to make for the imperative of investing in tomorrow's leaders today. It's the law of supply and demand: more organizations in greater competition under increased pressure to perform put a premium on scarce talent. The labor economy has become a seller's market, and poaching or luring talent away from other organizations is a losing proposition. The alternative is to become good at developing your talented managers into great leaders and aggressively seeking out potential and developing it anywhere and everywhere you can find it across the organization.

This defines an agenda for HR/OD&E and talent managers: creating integrated systems for churning out homegrown leaders. It's not enough to help individuals be effective in their current positions. We need talented managers ready to step into jobs of greater responsibility and hit the ground running. This is the challenge weighing on the talent profession today. With an urgent and daunting mandate, best-in-class talent managers have been courageously experimenting, curiously benchmarking, and feverishly seeking solutions.

The purpose of this volume is to share what has been learned in the last few years of increased attention to the systematic and strategic cultivation of leadership talent. The time is ripe for leading practitioners to share key lessons about building and filling a leadership pipeline.

The Audience for This Book

This collection of chapters was written expressly for those responsible for building leadership bench strength. The authors, all from internationally renowned consultancies and educational institutes, were asked to speak directly to senior human resources executives, organizational development and effectiveness directors, and consultants and trainers. The goal was to pass on lessons from experience. Each chapter is packed with practical advice and suggestions. At the same time, it is rigorously backed by scientific research, tested theory, and firsthand examples from Fortune 500 companies and major government organizations like the Central Intelligence Agency.

What follows, I think you will agree, is a collection of road-tested frameworks, strategies, and tactics that are useful in building your leadership pipeline. My reading of the five chapters suggests that each holds out the promise of at least one new "big idea" and a handful of specific action steps that flow naturally from it.

Structure and Content

This volume is divided into three parts, each corresponding to a particular perspective or set of considerations about building a leadership pipeline. These three perspectives are represented in figure 1. The basic idea is that there is a larger business environment shaping trends and offering examples to learn from. Within that larger context are your own particular organization and unique circumstances. On the one hand, you can consider your company's pool of talent, who these managers are as individuals, and what they need to realize their potential. On the other hand, you can look at the pipeline question from the perspective of development systems—the mechanics of talent development including processes, content, and tools for growing leaders. And there should be overlap between the individual and systems perspectives—effective talent development strategies are designed with both firmly in mind.

Rather than provide exhaustive coverage of each of the major considerations in figure 1, the focus of this volume is to provide targeted points of view relevant to each. The collection of chapters is also integrated; rather than submitting disparate papers to lump together, the authors have carefully

Figure 1. Key Considerations in Building a Leadership Pipeline

considered their contributions in light of what the other authors have to say. Based on the synergy and interconnectedness of the chapters, it seems evident that the authors found much to learn from each other.

Part 1: Business Environment

The first part frames the larger context of preparing for the leadership needs of the future with a chapter by Pat Weik of RHR International Company. Weik reports on a benchmarking survey summarizing current practices across 115 companies (most with greater than $1 billion in U.S. revenue) of preparing now for the future leadership of their enterprises. A key finding: filling the pipe is a new priority—most companies report ramping up the identification and focused development of high potentials only in the last three years. Weik also reports on the skills most sought after in high potentials, the roles senior leaders are playing, and key techniques facilitating accelerating development. Weik takes on the issue of impact: how are companies tracking investments in filling the pipe, assessing progress, and estimating ROI? Most are struggling with this. But there is hope: some companies are figuring it out.

Part 2: Considerations about Individual Managers

The next part includes two chapters that focus primarily on the needs of individual managers and leaders. First, Arthur Freedman of American University, National Training Labs Institute, and Quantum Associates describes a refined version of his "pathways-and-crossroads" model of how managers go from being frontline supervisors to CEOs. He considers how managerial jobs change across the hierarchy and how this poses a psychological challenge for ambitious, upwardly mobile individuals. Freedman describes how managers must reinvent themselves—by letting go of anachronistic skills, fine-tuning others, and picking up new skills and perspectives as they climb the corporate ladder. In addition to offering a practical psychology of moving through the leadership pipeline, he also identifies formal mechanisms that organizations can employ to prepare and support managers to make these moves. The chapter closes with an illustrating example of what is required of executives promoted to the role of CEO. Freedman's psychological model of the career pathways and crossroads was the subject of a paper voted article of the year for *Consulting Psychology Journal* in 1998.

Chapter 3 is a natural follow-up to Freedman's chapter; veteran consultants and authors Diane Downey and Amy Kates of Downey Kates Associates use a similar pathways-and-crossroads model to provide an in-depth treatment of general manager transitions. They also use Freedman's psychological model of managerial promotions to illustrate key sources of leverage for improving the success rate among newly promoted executives. This chapter provides an array of rich examples from the authors' considerable experience helping major companies like American Express, Wal-Mart, and Pfizer develop transition management and on-boarding programs. The chapter also includes a number of specific techniques and tools that can be readily adapted in your organization. One of the most compelling observations Downey and Kates offer is that, with few exceptions, successful techniques for helping leaders transition into more senior roles are fairly simple, low cost, and low tech. They are commonsense interventions, some of which you may be using. They see the greatest impact when these models are systematized, integrated, and woven into the cultural fabric of the company.

Part 3: Considerations about Development Systems

The final part includes two chapters relevant to the content, processes, and tools organizations use to develop talent. First, Skip Leonard of Personnel Decisions International builds on Freedman's pathways-and-crossroads model and makes an important point regarding the content of talent development efforts. From over twenty-five years of experience in dozens of organizations and with hundreds of managers at all levels, Leonard has made a striking observation: in the haste to turn every manager into a leader, fundamental management skills have been largely overlooked (for example, planning, delegation, follow-up, project management). The startling result is that senior executives regularly enter advanced leadership courses lacking the basic building blocks of management. He grounds this observation and his alternative recommendation in strong leadership theory—like John Kotter's classic distinction between leadership and management—as well as a great deal of statistical research on the distinction between transformational and transactional styles of leadership. Leonard's central message is that leadership development interventions need to be tailored to the particular organizational level and that adopting a "one best way" approach to development, although seductively simplifying, is ultimately shortsighted. Leonard concludes his chapter by helping HR/OD&E professionals take a more strategic approach to answering the question of ROI.

The fifth and final chapter in this volume is by Jennifer Martineau, Greg Laskow, and Lisa Moye of the Center for Creative Leadership, and their collaborator at the Central Intelligence Agency, Dick Phillips. They describe how they helped the CIA use leader development to transform its culture. In particular, they demonstrate a fully integrated approach to creating a competency system for all levels of management. The system contains both consistent themes that cut across all layers of management as well as unique themes that capture the particular challenges facing supervisors, middle managers, and executives. The case vividly illustrates design principles, strategies, and tactics for building a model of leadership that serves as the central architecture guiding all leader development initiatives. They show how this "customized integration" competency model specifies the content of training and development, provides a basis for receiving 360-degree feedback, and identifies the metrics for evaluating impact, the ROI in leadership development.

Final Comments

It is an honorable challenge to be responsible for ensuring your organization's continuity and sustainability by preparing the next generations of leaders. May you find much to pick from in the following buffet of essential insights from respected practitioners. It is our highest hope that this volume will provide you with practical suggestions, creative ideas, and inspiration for new initiatives.

I would like to thank the Center for Creative Leadership, long a pioneer in the development of leaders, for providing this forum, in which the field's leading institutions can pool together their collective wisdom for the benefit of those charged with the responsibility of building the leaders of tomorrow.

Building the Executive Ranks:
Current Practices in Developing Future Business Leaders

Patricia M. Weik
RHR International Company

If there is an emerging constant on the business horizon, it is that companies can expect to face a world of increasing complexity, uncertainty, and competitive pressure. As businesses prepare themselves strategically for this future, some companies—from market leaders like Gillette and Best Buy to small professional firms and local chambers of commerce—have put a sharp focus on increasing their supply of leaders capable of meeting these challenges. These forward-thinking organizations are learning through real-time applications about what works and, just as important, what doesn't in the race to build leadership capacity.

RHR International Company is a firm of management psychologists who have been consulting with current and future leaders of companies around the globe for sixty years. We designed the ExecutiveBench Research Program[1] (see exhibit 1.1, page 8) to identify emerging practices in the development of future leaders. Like most benchmarking efforts, we wanted to identify new, innovative models and practices that others might find useful. And we also were interested in identifying areas for improvement—those practices that companies are struggling to effectively implement. In this chapter, I describe the multiphase research effort and present key findings we discovered in the first phase, including a summary of the current state of executive bench strength and best practices in the identification and development of future leaders.

This chapter is structured around four key areas of inquiry. First, we examine the emerging state of the talent market. Here we address questions such as the following: How concerned are companies about the changes in the talent market? How many senior leaders are expected to depart in the next five years? How confident are companies that they can meet their future growth needs by developing leaders?

The second key area this chapter treats concerns how prepared companies are to meet future needs for leadership. This section covers questions such as the following: How effective are companies' development programs for future leaders? What is the commitment of senior management to growing future leaders?

Exhibit 1.1. Key Findings from the RHR International Company Benchmarking Study

- Most companies are not very confident in their ability to meet future growth needs.
- In most companies talent development is still considered to be a project or program, not a way of doing business.
- Organizations want leaders who have the courage to make the right decisions and who get business done by building strong relationships and inspiring others to drive necessary change.
- Managers of future leaders will play a critical role in development, but most companies are not prepared to fully leverage this resource.
- Uncovering best practices continues to be a challenge, in part because most companies still struggle to measure the effectiveness of their current leadership development practices.

The third area under consideration is best practices that are evolving in the identification and development of future leaders, as well as areas for improvement. We address these questions: What characteristics are companies looking for in their leaders? How are future leaders being identified? How do companies communicate with future leaders (and others)? What experiences have been found to be most important in growing future leaders?

Finally, the last area of inquiry is how to assess the impact and calculate the value added from investments in the future. How are companies measuring the effectiveness of their development processes? And how is the value to the company ascertained?

The ExecutiveBench Research Program

Research Goals

A growing body of literature published over the past decade has focused on how companies successfully grow leaders for the long term. The McKinsey report, "The War for Talent" (Chambers, Foulon, Handfield-Jones, Hankin, & Michaels, 1998), makes the case that high-performing companies consistently develop and reward their highest-performing employees, while

*High Flyer*s (McCall, 1998), *The Leadership Pipeline* (Charan, Drotter, & Noel, 2001), and *Voice of the Leader* (Corporate Leadership Council, 2001) explore, among other issues, what experiences best prepare young managers for the increased responsibility of senior leadership. At RHR International, our direct experience in consulting with hundreds of companies of all sizes has confirmed what the literature suggests: companies are taking very seriously the issue of developing future leaders and making it a strategic priority.

As companies are focusing increasingly on talent development, they are asking for guidance as to the best practices in developing leaders with high potential. And their questions about best practices are becoming more specific: How many individuals should be in a development program? How should they be selected? Do you tell them they are on a high potential list? The research I describe in this chapter was designed to answer questions like these in a systematic and reliable manner. We wanted to find out just how companies are managing the development of their future leaders, from design through execution. In particular, we wanted to know how practices are evolving (and what practices are most effective) and where companies are still struggling to effectively grow the next generation of leaders.

Research Design

Phase 1 of the research consisted of a survey of current practices in the selection and development of future leaders. Since we were looking for fairly detailed information about current development practices, we knew that the length of the survey could be a problem. We piloted two different versions of the survey in the spring of 2003. One pilot survey was administered at a *Business Week* conference cosponsored by RHR International. The other pilot survey was administered at the annual meeting of an international trade association. The pilot questions were evaluated for clarity and for the utility of the responses they generated. We rolled out the final ExecutiveBench Survey in October 2003, administering the survey both online and in hard copy. The target audience for the survey included senior line executives, senior human resources executives, and HR and organizational development professionals responsible for leadership development.

As of April 2004, 115 companies had completed the survey. The research results that follow are based on analyses of those 115 respondents. Phase 2 of the research, which began in October 2004, involves a series of follow-up interviews with a subset of the companies that responded to the survey. The interviews are designed to understand how companies' development practices evolve over time and how the current leaders and organizational culture shape the choices companies make in refining and augmenting those practices. At the time of this writing, data collection is still in progress for Phase 2, so we are unable to report those findings in full here. Where possible, I will draw on preliminary data from the interviews to further inform the results from Phase 1, the survey of the 115 companies.

Research Sample

The 115 respondents to the ExecutiveBench Survey came from nineteen different industries.[2] The majority of the companies, about 90 percent, were based in the United States. But over half of these U.S. companies had significant international business operations. In terms of company size, responses were fairly evenly distributed between companies over $1 billion in annual revenue (54 percent) and under $1 billion (46 percent). About a quarter (27 percent) of companies reported revenues under $200 million, 19 percent reported revenues between $200 million and $1 billion, 34 percent reported revenues between $1 billion and $10 billion, and 20 percent reported revenues over $10 billion. It appears to be a fairly representative sample of American businesses.

Individual respondents came from a variety of backgrounds, with the largest proportion of respondents (43 percent) being senior vice presidents of human resources. CEOs comprised 20 percent of the respondents, while other senior line executives made up 22 percent of the sample. HR/organizational development professionals below the level of senior vice president made up 15 percent of the sample. All in all, we were satisfied that our informants were in a strong position to comment on their company's practices.

Findings from the Study

State of the Talent Market

Although the popular press and, to a lesser extent, some consulting companies have been warning of a looming talent shortage, just how seriously senior managers are taking this threat has been less clear. Is this a burning issue to business leaders or some vague, ethereal concern about the distant future? We wanted to go beyond case examples and assess how much of a talent shortage companies across the board are anticipating. Thus, one section of the ExecutiveBench Survey explores how current leaders view their bench strength, the role of retirements at the top, and their level of concern around having the talent to meet their future growth needs.

The overall picture of projected leadership needs through 2010 is a sobering one (see figure 1.1). Companies anticipate significant departures within the senior management ranks (defined as the two levels below the CEO) by the year 2010. Half of the companies reported that they expect to lose 50 percent or more of their senior managers, while 15 percent said they expect to lose 75 percent or more of their senior managers.

Figure 1.1. Anticipated Departures of Senior-Level Executives

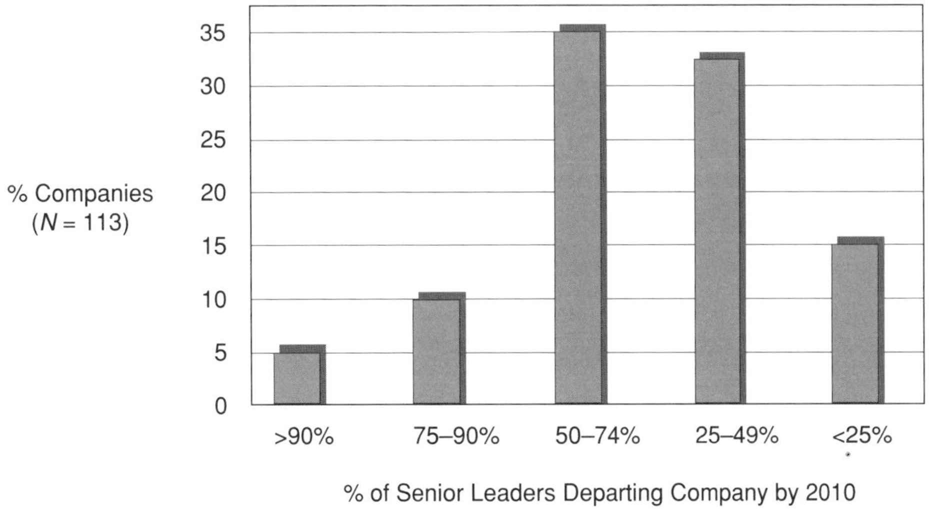

% Companies ($N = 113$)

% of Senior Leaders Departing Company by 2010

Virtually all companies are relying to some extent on outside hires to replace departing managers (see figure 1.2). By far the largest proportion of companies, or 41 percent of respondents, reported that they expect to hire one-quarter to one-half of their leaders from outside over the next five to seven years. In addition, 60 percent of companies expect to hire at least 25 percent of their leaders from outside. It appears that companies are looking externally for talent at a somewhat increasing rate: a 1998 study by the Center for Creative Leadership reported that only about 30 to 40 percent of all executive placements were recruited from outside the hiring company (Sessa, Kaiser, Taylor, & Campbell, 1998).

Figure 1.2. Anticipated Hires of Outside Leaders

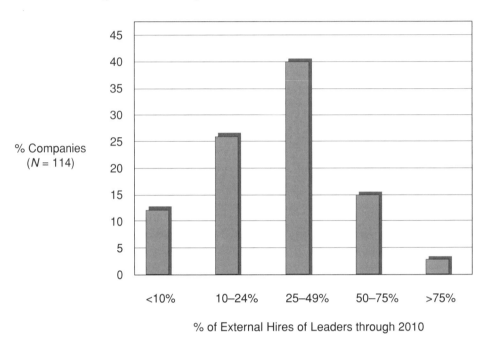

% Companies
(*N* = 114)

% of External Hires of Leaders through 2010

It is unclear whether companies regard the increased reliance on outside hires as a good thing. Many companies struggle to know what is the "right" level of turnover for bringing in innovative ideas and needed strategic or culture change. The ExecutiveBench Survey attempted to shed light in this area by measuring the level of concern about a potential talent shortage. Companies were asked how confident they were that they would have sufficient high potential talent to meet their future growth needs. Only 25 percent of companies reported that they were highly confident in their ability to meet their future growth needs with high potentials. The remaining 75 percent were only "somewhat confident" or "not at all confident" about the state of their internal capacity to meet future leadership demands.[3]

Moreover, when the relationships between expected losses of senior leaders, anticipated numbers of outside hires, and confidence levels were jointly examined, a consistent pattern emerged. The number of senior leadership departures through 2010 and the number of anticipated outside hires were also both significantly correlated with confidence levels (Spearman's rho = .262 and .330 respectively, $p < .01$).

Thus, companies that expect more senior leader departures and also anticipate having to rely on outside hires to replace senior leaders are the least confident that they will be able to meet future growth needs. These companies do not appear satisfied with the greater reliance on outside hires to fill key roles. And perhaps for good reason: the CCL study cited earlier found that external hires are much less likely to be successful than internal hires under a range of common conditions like highly volatile industries, when industry and product knowledge is vital, and in organizations with firmly rooted cultures (Sessa et al., 1998). This suggests that the anticipated mass changing of the guard at the top of companies will likely bring significant change and discontinuity as seasoned leaders depart and are replaced by a combination of less seasoned insiders and new external hires.

Figure 1.3. Company Confidence That High Potential Talent Will Address Future Growth Needs

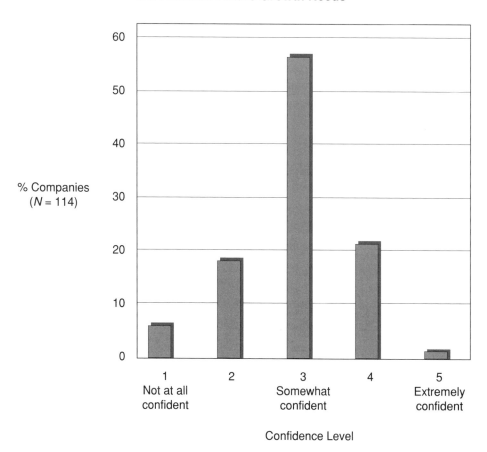

% Companies ($N = 114$)

Confidence Level

Level of Preparedness for the Future

Experience building bench strength. Another goal of the ExecutiveBench Survey was to understand how prepared companies are to meet the challenges of managing and growing key talent. The survey explored how long companies have been formally identifying and developing future leaders. We found that formal attendance to the growth of future leaders is a fairly recent practice for most companies, with 57 percent reporting that they have been identifying and developing future leaders for less than three years. The most frequently endorsed response was "1 to 3 years," with 31 percent of companies endorsing this response.

Company size seems to matter (see figure 1.4). Companies with over $1 billion in revenues have, on average, been developing future leaders longer than smaller companies. For example, of the twenty-two companies that have been identifying and developing future leaders for seven years or longer, 64 percent were companies with over $1 billion in revenue.

Figure 1.4. Longevity of Formal Development Programs for Future Leaders

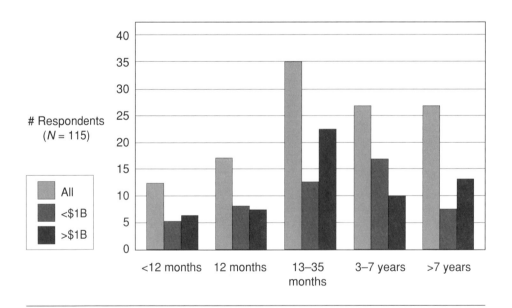

Senior management commitment to future leaders. The commitment of the senior executive team is particularly crucial when building sustainable talent development programs. Identifying and developing high potential talent is by its nature a long-term proposition that is unlikely to reach fruition without the firm endorsement and support of senior management. In addition, future leaders are by definition company resources that the senior team needs to understand in order to make wise decisions in terms of future assignments. And at some point the development needs of future leaders will aggregate around broader and higher-level abilities like strategic thinking and planning and managing cross-functional teams from a distance, and senior leaders will be needed to coach and mentor future leaders in these key areas.

When asked what roles the senior team plays in the identification and development of future leaders (see exhibit 1.2), by far the most frequently endorsed activity (91 percent) was the identification of individuals with high potential. (In comparison, the second most endorsed activity, at 69 percent, was defining the leadership abilities needed in future leaders based on the business strategy.) Since, in many companies, future leaders may be positioned several levels below the senior team, the question emerges of how well the senior managers actually know their future leaders. In some companies, the senior team devotes a great deal of time to talent roundtables where potential future leaders are discussed regularly and in detail. In other firms, senior leaders are regularly assigned as mentors to younger managers with high potential. However, it is unlikely that these practices are utilized by 90 percent of companies (since, for example, only 67 percent of respondents said that their senior leaders coach and mentor future leaders). If many senior leaders do not have direct exposure to their high potentials, the question becomes this: How else are executives gathering reliable and credible data about future leaders? This is a topic that will be covered in more detail in Phase 2 of the research program. Preliminary results from the interviews point to two additional areas: some companies develop future leaders using action-learning projects (Marquardt, 2004) that involve senior leaders as advisors or sponsors; other companies invite future leaders to off-site meetings or other events carefully designed so that senior leaders can get to know them in a social setting.

We found that senior leaders generally are playing an active role early in the development process. In addition to identifying high potentials, 65 percent of companies said their senior leaders allocate resources for future-leader development, and 63 percent make future-leader development a strategic priority. However, only 46 percent of respondents reported that their

Exhibit 1.2. The Senior Team's Role in Future-Leader Development

Q: What roles do you and your senior team play in the identification and develop-ment of your company's future leaders?
(Percentage of companies that endorsed each activity, *N* = 115)

• Identify individuals with high potential	91%
• Define leadership abilities based on strategy	69%
• One-on-one coaching or mentoring	67%
• Allocate resources for leadership development	65%
• Make development of talent a strategic priority	63%
• Hold others accountable for talent development	46%
• Select external leadership development partners	39%
• Uncover stretch roles	38%
• Other	6%

senior managers hold others accountable for talent development. This result suggests that while many companies are increasing their focus on talent development, far fewer have figured out how to weave the practice into their cultural fabric as a way of doing business. This result may be due largely to the fact that growing future leaders is a fairly recent priority. In companies that have been identifying and developing future leaders longer, senior leaders are more involved in growing their future leaders, as evidenced by the positive correlation between longevity of formal programs with the endorse-ment of a greater total number of development activities performed by senior management (Spearman's rho = .358, $p < .01$).

In the future, as future-leader development practices mature, it is likely that senior leaders will be more involved with growing the next generation. Companies that report greater involvement by senior management in develop-ing future leaders also report a higher level of confidence in their ability to meet future growth needs by drawing on high potential talent (Spearman's rho = .221, $p < .05$). Thus, it seems clear that the active involvement and commitment by senior management is pivotal to building a deep pool of talent.

Practices in Identifying and Developing Future Leaders

Commonly sought characteristics. The overall picture of what companies are looking for in their future leaders suggests a melding of traditional individual strengths—like courage to make the right decisions (75 percent of companies endorsed) and decisiveness (60 percent endorsed)—with a more nimble, relational style. When asked what characteristics they look for when identifying and developing future leaders, the number one response was the ability to build strong relationships internally and externally (86 percent), closely followed by openness to change and growth (81 percent).[4] In contrast, only 57 percent emphasized the ability to identify and develop talent, reinforcing the idea presented earlier that talent development is not necessarily a core value or a strategic priority, even in companies that are seeking to improve their ability to grow future leaders. Only 45 percent of respondents emphasized superior intellectual abilities in their future leaders, an interesting and somewhat puzzling result given the increasing complexity of the global business environment. This result will be explored in more detail in Phase 2 of the research.

Exhibit 1.3. What Companies Look for in Their Future Leaders
(Percentage of companies that endorsed each ability, *N* = 111)

- Ability to build strong relationships internally and externally — 86%
- Openness to change and growth — 81%
- Courage to make the right decisions — 75%
- Ability to motivate and inspire others — 75%
- Level of self-confidence — 70%
- Awareness of one's own strengths and limitations — 68%
- Personal desire to succeed — 68%
- Commitment to the success of the business, even when personal sacrifice is involved — 67%
- A core set of leadership values that the individual lives by — 67%
- Broad, comprehensive knowledge of the business — 65%
- Decisiveness — 60%
- Ability to identify and develop talent — 57%
- Superior intellectual abilities — 45%
- Other — 12%

Identifying future leaders. Nearly two-thirds (62 percent) of companies reported that they tell individuals they are perceived to have high potential, but many respondents qualified this statement by adding that the conversations happen informally and inconsistently. Of the many issues companies are grappling with in this area, how to communicate to the organization that certain individuals have been targeted as future leaders is apparently one of the most daunting. Some companies fear they will inflate the expectations of talented managers and then disappoint them. Others are concerned about anointing heirs apparent, who then may grow complacent and lose their drive to succeed. Still others are concerned about demoralizing solid performers who are not identified. These concerns are often exacerbated when the company culture is highly egalitarian (so no one is "special") or where employees do not often get direct performance feedback. Managers of future leaders are key to this feedback process, but our early investigation suggests that companies do not prepare their managers adequately to communicate the right, balanced message to future leaders and also to engage in real dialogue with them about their career interests, family and personal needs, and all of the other issues related to advancement and assuming more significant responsibilities. (See also chapter 2 for reasons that organizations tend to be naive about what it means for individuals to climb the corporate ladder.)

Developing future leaders. In developing future leaders, companies rely heavily on internal resources, particularly the managers of those future leaders. An actively involved boss was the most important development resource, cited by 84 percent of companies. The second most important experience was stretch assignments (endorsed by 71 percent of companies), followed by mentoring and internal coaching with senior executives. Peer contact and feedback, in contrast, were endorsed by less than half of the companies, both of which are experiences that the *Voice of the Leader* research (Corporate Leadership Council, 2001) suggested up-and-coming leaders value and would like to have more of. Stretch assignments and actively involved bosses were also the experiences rated as being most effective in developing future leaders. Development assessments by outside consultants ranked third in effectiveness, even though only half of the companies reported using such assessments as part of the development process.

Larger companies, on average, tend to use a greater variety of development experiences to grow future leaders (Spearman's rho = .315, $p < .01$). Thus, while larger companies have a more diversified portfolio of development interventions, there is not a great deal of difference in the kinds of

Exhibit 1.4. Experiences That Companies Rely on to Develop Future Leaders

(Percentage of companies that endorsed each activity, $N = 105$)

• Actively involved boss	84%
• New, significant roles that stretch individual	71%
• Mentoring relationships with senior executives	70%
• Coaching relationships within company	67%
• External executive education programs	67%
• Formal development planning	67%
• In-house executive education programs	54%
• Use of outside-the-company coaches	52%
• Development assessments by outside consultants	51%
• Peer contact and feedback	48%
• Rigorous monitoring of progress against development goals	41%
• Other	4%

experiences smaller and larger companies rely upon. In terms of what does distinguish these two, our early interviews suggested that larger companies rely on internal executive education and formal action-learning projects more frequently than do smaller companies. Companies that use a greater variety of experiences in developing their leaders are also more confident that these leaders will meet their future growth needs (see exhibit 1.5; Spearman's rho = .205, $p < .05$). Providing a greater diversity of experiences to future leaders may prove effective on two fronts: First, it suggests that companies are tailoring the experiences to the individuals (that is, there is no boilerplate plan that is being applied to all future leaders). Second, it suggests that individual future leaders are being developed through a variety of methods in order to develop a greater breadth of skills, perspectives, and abilities.

Measuring Impact and Value

As noted in chapter 4, the question of impact or return on investment is important to those responsible for leadership development. Respondents generally reported having difficulty in measuring the effectiveness of development experiences. Only 41 percent of companies, for example, relied on rigorous monitoring of development goals. And our preliminary interviews of

Exhibit 1.5. The Perceived Effectiveness of Development Experiences

(Average rated effectiveness of each activity where 1 = ineffective
and 5 = extremely effective)

• Developmental, stretch assignments within company	3.9
• Involved boss	3.7
• Development assessments by outside consultants	3.5
• In-house executive education programs	3.4
• Formal development planning	3.4
• Mentoring relationships with senior executives	3.4
• Use of outside-the-company coaches	3.3
• Coaching relationships within company	3.3
• Rigorous monitoring of progress against development goals	3.2
• External executive education programs	3.1
• Peer contact and feedback	3.1

HR professionals suggest that rigorous follow-up to assess whether development plans are being executed is not currently a common component of future-leader programs. Nor do companies systematically track how their leaders change or progress as a result of development experiences.

Any analysis of ROI has to begin with measuring the actual impact of the development intervention. When asked in the survey, "How should organizations measure ROI when deciding to invest in the development of future leaders?" more than half of the respondents did not answer or reported that they did not know the answer. The next most frequently reported response was retention of future leaders, the impact of which respondents said could be measured in the reduction of the numbers of leaders hired away by other companies. Companies reported measuring the value of retaining future leaders in terms of reductions in the costs of recruiting replacement leaders. They did not attempt to measure the value of keeping leaders in terms of opportunity costs, such as the increased operational efficiencies resulting from avoiding having key positions vacant for a period of time, or minimizing the timeline for integrating outside hires. (See chapter 3 for the extra time it takes to assimilate an external hire.) Promotion of future leaders into key roles was the next most frequently mentioned way to measure ROI, followed by shorter learning curves for the future leaders when they are promoted into new key roles, and fewer costly mistakes as they learned the ropes in new roles.

A content analysis of all responses to the open-ended ROI question suggests a pattern of thinking in organizations about ROI that may be overly constricted. Companies appear to be searching for metrics that are closely tied to direct, bottom-line measures and that are also clearly tied to the individuals being affected, that is, the future leaders. When both of those criteria are applied, however, the universe of possible metrics quickly becomes fairly narrowly focused on replacement costs. Such a talent-accounting scheme does not account for opportunity losses or larger, systemic costs to the organization as a whole. Moreover, this cost accounting only considers head count. It fails to acknowledge the competitive advantages that come with improving leadership capacity, which may be the ultimate driver that spurs companies to invest in their talent (see Barrick, Day, Lord, & Alexander, 1991; Porter, 1985; Zenger & Folkman, 2002).

However, a few pioneering companies are making headway on the ROI question, largely through a willingness to accept relevant but nontraditional metrics. A couple of respondents mentioned enhanced reputation in the marketplace for being a good employer to work for, which presumably would increase their ability to hire desirable employees. Another company cited improved ability of future leaders to develop talent below them, thus creating a true leadership pipeline with replacement candidates at every level.

Nine respondents said that the ROI question is unnecessary because the value of talent development is self-evident. Although this number represented a small percentage of respondents, it is worth mentioning because eight of the nine respondents were CEOs. Their responses are a timely reminder, particularly to HR professionals who are working to create credible development programs that have staying power, that there may be no right answer to the question of measuring the value of talent development. The choice of meaningful metrics and how they are interpreted is always closely linked to the organizational culture and to the values of senior leaders.

Conclusion

If your company is new to the realm of future-leader development, you are not alone. Many companies are new entrants looking to catch up quickly. Key lessons from our research suggest that successful programs start with committed senior managers who own and drive the development of future leaders.

Development programs need not be highly structured and formal, but they should be aligned with the strategy and culture of the company. In terms of development experiences, future leaders need diversity, stretch, and the involvement of bosses and other seasoned veterans. And follow-through on development plans is critical, both to ensure that execution of plans actually happens and to assess the impact of the experiences that get implemented. Yet current practice is lagging on follow-through.

There is an old African proverb that says the best time to plant a tree is twenty years ago. The second best time is today. Whatever ground must be laid in your company to make leadership development happen, begin planting today.

Notes

1. ExecutiveBench is a trademark, owned and registered by RHR International Company.

2. The industries represented include automotive, chambers of commerce, chemicals, consumer products, education, energy, entertainment/media, financial services, food/food services, health care, insurance, manufacturing, pharmaceutical, professional services, publishing, retail, telecom, technology, and transportation.

3. The answer to the question of what is the right amount of turnover is closely linked to the strategy and culture of a company; therefore, providing a definitive number can be problematic. Companies going through significant strategic shifts may need to import a larger number of outside leaders to provide the new skills required by the new strategy. Companies with a highly complex strategy or a deeply imbedded, long-standing culture may find it more difficult to assimilate outsiders. Given the complexity of the issue, RHR decided to tackle the problem from a couple of different directions. First, we decided to take a longitudinal perspective, believing that best practices should be derived not by just examining the practices of financially sound businesses (probably the most common way of delineating best practices) but by examining the practices of strong businesses that have withstood the test of time. In our view, companies may demonstrate multiple quarters of strong financial performance for a variety of reasons; these companies, particularly if they are still experimenting with future-leader development, may not be the standard bearers in this area. As is noted above, our research suggests that many companies are newcomers to the realm of future-leader development, and accordingly, the picture of best practices is in some ways still emerging. Phase 2 of this research will focus specifically on high-performing companies that have been formally developing future leaders over several years and that have been assessing the efficacy of their programs.

4. It is interesting to note that a recent CCL study that asked up-and-coming leaders what competencies they were most interested in developing found that interpersonal skills and strategic-thinking skills also topped the list (Deal & DePinto, 2004). Thus, it appears that organizations and high potentials are in synch to a certain extent about what mission-critical competencies provide a competitive advantage.

References

Barrick, M. R., Day, D. V., Lord, R. G., & Alexander, R. A. (1991). Assessing the utility of executive leadership. *Leadership Quarterly, 2,* 9–22.

Chambers, E. G., Foulon, M., Handfield-Jones, H., Hankin, S. M., & Michaels, E. G., III. (1998). The war for talent. *The McKinsey Quarterly, 3,* 44–57.

Charan, R., Drotter, S., & Noel, J. (2001). *The leadership pipeline: How to build the leadership-powered company.* San Francisco: Jossey-Bass.

Corporate Leadership Council. (2001). *Voice of the leader: A quantitative analysis of leadership bench strength and development strategies.* Washington, DC: Corporate Executive Board.

Deal, J. J., & DePinto, R. (2004, April). Differences in the developmental needs of managers at multiple levels. In R. B. Kaiser & S. B. Craig (Cochairs), *Filling the pipe I: Studying management development across the hierarchy.* Symposium presented at the Nineteenth Annual Conference of the Society for Industrial and Organizational Psychology, Chicago.

Marquardt, M. J. (2004). *Action learning: Solving problems and building leaders in real time.* Palo Alto, CA: Davies-Black Publishing.

McCall, M. W., Jr. (1998). *High flyers: Developing the next generation of leaders.* Boston: Harvard Business School Press.

Porter, M. (1985). *Competitive advantage: Creating and sustaining superior performance.* New York: Free Press.

Sessa, V. I., Kaiser, R., Taylor, J. K., & Campbell, R. J. (1998). *Executive selection: A research report on what works and what doesn't.* Greensboro, NC: Center for Creative Leadership.

Zenger, J. H., & Folkman, J. (2002). *The extraordinary leader: Turning good managers into great leaders.* New York: McGraw-Hill.

Swimming Upstream:
The Challenge of Managerial Promotions

Arthur M. Freedman
American University, NTL Institute, and Quantum Associates

On the surface, promotions sound like a good thing—especially for driven high achievers bent on making something of their careers. But like most things in life, the reality is far less glamorous than the cover story. In truth, promotions to jobs of greater responsibility, prestige, and influence are among the most difficult challenges one will face over the course of a career. There is much suspense: Will the person hit the ground running? Will he or she flounder? And much is at stake: Will the organization continue smoothly, or will there be disruption? Will the individual become a more mature leader, or will he or she get stuck in old routines?

In this chapter, I describe why promotions are so challenging and suggest how to help individual managers cope with the difficulties in making an upward transition. The chapter concludes with applying this perspective to the transition from executive leader of a portfolio of businesses to the leader of an institution as chief executive officer. The next chapter deals with the unique transition into general management.

Pathways and Crossroads

"Leadership pipeline" models have become popular for characterizing how the managerial job changes dramatically as you ascend the hierarchy. For instance, the best-selling book *The Leadership Pipeline* (Charan, Drotter, & Noel, 2001) contains one such framework. These models trace back to the work of Walter Mahler and William Wrightnour (1973), who were among the first to describe how a few leading corporations like General Electric and Exxon were approaching the replacement of key executives. Over the last ten years, dozens of other organizations have adopted their general ideas about how the managerial job changes across organizational levels.

In 1998, I described a pathways-and-crossroads model of managerial careers inspired by this work but emphasizing the psychology of an upward promotion. In that paper, I assert: "When upwardly mobile persons are promoted from lower, individual contributor roles to higher, managerial roles, they are confronted by the challenge of negotiating a series of 135-degree 'crossroads' or shifts in their careers. For those who make the complete journey, they must traverse five pathways and four crossroads. These critical career crossroads are comprised of discontinuous and unprecedented changes in the role responsibilities . . . which managers-in-transition must [perform]. At each crossroad, people are confronted by a triple challenge: letting go of anachronistic responsibilities and competencies; preserving those that continue to be useful; and adding on new, discontinuous responsibilities and consequences. Managers-in-transition can cope with these demands by making adaptive changes in their preferred activities, behavior patterns, and style" (Freedman, 1998, p. 131).

Summarizing briefly, the four crossroads are (1) from individual contributor to supervisory manager, (2) from supervisory manager to manager of a single "business,"[1] (3) from manager of a single "business" to executive manager of a portfolio of several "businesses," and (4) from executive manager of several "businesses" to institutional leader. A graphic depiction of this model is presented in figure 2.1. Rather than focus on how the nature of work substantively changes across levels, I emphasize the unique psychological challenges confronting managers-in-transition. There are several resources available to those interested in how the nature of managerial work changes with hierarchical level (for example, Charan et al., 2001; Freedman, 1998; Zaccaro, 2001).

Promotable, ambitious managers-in-transition must bridge unprecedented discontinuities at each of these four crossroads to reach the senior leader position. They must recognize and respond in an acceptable manner to the unique demands and role responsibilities of each higher-level position. To ensure their effectiveness, they must be ready to alter their beliefs, perspectives, attitudes, relationships, and behavior patterns at each crossroad.

On the Folly of "Sink or Swim"

A critical question is how ambitious, upwardly mobile managers become aware of, accept as legitimate, and develop proficiency in applying new perspectives, values, and skills that are often quite different from those that brought them prior success. In spite of Henry Mintzberg's (1994) admonitions, traditional and executive MBA programs omit the critical behavioral aspects of leadership from their core curricula. So the answer isn't found in business schools.

**Figure 2.1. The Five Primary Pathways and
Four Basic Career Crossroads**

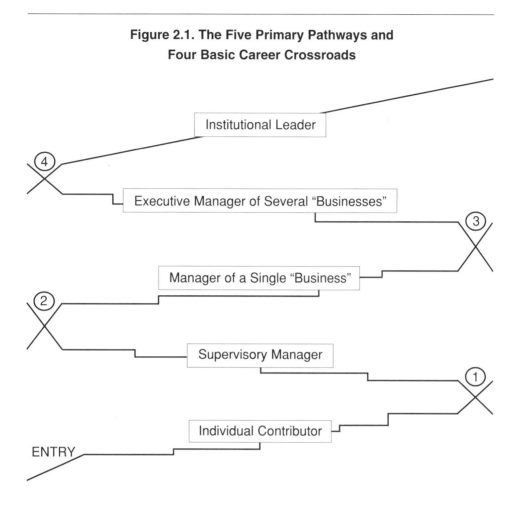

Note. Within each of the five pathways, the vertical risers imply rotation among related positions or progression along any given career pathway.

According to recent surveys, few organizations feel as if they do a good job of preparing upwardly mobile persons to assume more senior roles (see chapter 1). According to my forty-five-plus years of consulting with dozens of large and small corporations in all sectors, it seems that the way most companies handle this rests on the implicit belief that it is acceptable, if not appropriate, for newly promoted managers to either sink or swim in their new roles. Responsibility for making the transition successfully appears to be left to the managers themselves; in many cases, the organization assumes little, if any, responsibility.

This approach makes for an inefficient talent management strategy, made worse by the modern era of scarce talent. A much more effective strategy is for organizations to assume the lion's share of responsibility for upward transitions; they must create strategies, processes, and mechanisms to actively manage conditions that enable high potential managers-in-transition to traverse the four crossroads in figure 2.1. To do this, organizations must develop the capability to enable, support, and provide incentives for such upwardly mobile individuals to

- understand where they fit within their organization's executive continuity and leadership succession plans;

- develop realistic career goals and plans for achieving them;

- identify personal and systemic obstacles to fulfilling increasingly demanding leadership roles and prepare themselves to change—to learn and in many instances to unlearn;

- take advantage of relevant executive education, training, and developmental opportunities, prior to being promoted, that will prepare them to assume higher-level organizational positions;

- take advantage of coaching and mentoring resources.

Unless organizations properly and realistically prepare them, managers-in-transition are likely to assume that traversing a promotional crossroad will be an easy transition rather than the challenging, discontinuous transformation that research has continually shown it to require (for example, Charan et al., 2001; Downey, March, & Berkman, 2001; Freedman, 1998; McCall, Lombardo, & Morrison, 1988).

The Psychological Challenge

Major upward transitions move managers out of their comfort zone. Promotions trigger strong emotions that naturally arise as managers-in-transition realize that the demands made of them at higher organizational levels differ in kind from those that were made of them when they held lower-level positions. Under the surface, this challenge often threatens managers-in-transition. It can undermine their sense of coherence and well-being—critical components of self-esteem and confidence that are weakened by the loss of psychic anchors, such as their competent performance of public roles (Freedman, 1995b). This is to say that managers-in-transition gradually discover that opportunities to perform their familiar, well-practiced, public roles as individual contributors or lower-level managers are drastically reduced or entirely lost as they work their way upward.

Initially, managers-in-transition often feel adrift—isolated and alone. Too often, they are both unfamiliar with and unskilled in performing their new tasks, activities, and functions. Their dawning awareness of this discontinuity often triggers a sense of intense discomfort and insecurity. They frequently speak of feeling hollow—empty and without purpose or value. They may feel like frauds who have deceived themselves, those who promoted them, and those who now depend upon them. Not that all of this is public knowledge. I've come to learn about this phenomenon in my intensely personal consulting experience with individual executives. These managers-in-transition aren't comfortable with such feelings and mask them from their coworkers. But that they aren't obvious doesn't mean these powerful emotions are not at play; they are real and they do have a significant impact on executive performance.

Managers-in-transition typically require at least six months of post-transition experience to recognize, accept, and develop reasonable proficiency in performing their new role responsibilities (Freedman, 1998; Gabarro, 1987). It may even take up to a full eighteen months for most managers to feel emotionally confident in a new role (Downey et al., 2001; see also chapter 3).[2] All too often, organizations neither recognize nor dedicate necessary and sufficient resources to adequately prepare or support them through the intellectual and emotional learning curves. Managers-in-transition are likely to be left on their own. They may realize their existing skill sets are inadequate in coping with their unprecedented leadership responsibilities and may sense the need for assistance to adapt and cope effectively with the demands of their new roles. However, too often they will not act on that realization because they fear that requests for assistance may be construed as an admission of some personal defect, deficiency, or inadequacy.

To compensate for feeling inadequate, new managers often regress to performing familiar lower-level managerial or technical responsibilities that used to lead to recognition and approval. Unfortunately, these are now their subordinates' responsibilities; to persist in performing them simply does not satisfy the new demands of the higher-level managerial roles (Freedman, 1995a). As an example, Kaplan and Kaiser (2003) describe the common case of freshly minted senior executives who misallocate time and energy by delving into operational detail and diverting attention from the more central strategic aspects of their new job. Not only does this rob the organization of strategic leadership, but it also can be maddening and alienating to the new leader's subordinates, who feel untrusted and micromanaged.

Managers-in-transition must develop an understanding of when and how their circumstances have changed. They must learn to recognize when they are confronted by a major career crossroad. They must discern the new, unprecedented, mostly discontinuous but legitimate and demanding requirements of their new career pathway. They must recognize that some of their existing competencies will be required on their new pathway after they have traversed their next higher crossroad—and these must be preserved. But the relevance of many other competencies will be lost. They must learn to let go of these anachronisms quickly—with respect and appreciation for their historical relevance and contributions—and then move on. And they must identify and add on (that is, acquire proficiency in applying) at least a few new, radically different competencies and attributes to perform their new responsibilities and cope with and satisfy the demanding requirements of their new roles.

Why Managers Get Stuck

The irony is that upwardly promoted managers are leaving jobs they are likely to be better qualified to effectively perform than the ones they are entering. These old, familiar roles have provided opportunities to practice and develop competence. With sufficient repetitions, competence then leads to confidence in both the skills they have mastered and in themselves more fundamentally. In turn, they become comfortable in performing their role responsibilities. The result of this cycle of the three Cs—competence, confidence, and comfort—is an enhanced sense of pride and self-esteem.

Understandably, many people like these good feelings that come with the three Cs. Unfortunately, many rely on these good feelings to the point that they addict themselves to whatever results in recognition, achievement, and success. The corollary is that addicted persons pay an opportunity cost: to the extent that they continue to perform anachronistic roles to which they have addicted themselves, they will not create opportunities for themselves to even attempt to identify and master the new competencies and to perform the new role responsibilities that their discontinuous, higher-level positions may require. To let go of addictive but outmoded performances is often experienced as a tremendous loss—the loss of habitual sources of social reinforcement. As with addiction to drugs, alcohol, and tobacco, it is very difficult to let go and experience the pain of loss and withdrawal.

Leaders who are unaware of their behavioral addictions—that is, leaders who lack self-awareness—are most likely to act in ways that are self-defeating. They "shoot themselves in the foot" and often displace blame onto others for interfering with their ability to deal with new challenges, even though they are the ones who choose to use their anachronistic competencies. When they are confronted with unfamiliar challenges, they intensify their habitual ways of coping by applying their historically useful but no longer relevant competencies ("I don't know how to do this, so I'll do more of what I do know"). New circumstances, conditions, events, and situations become threats to such people. Over time and without modification, anachronistic coping patterns become the addicted person's primary but flawed means of coping with anything new—and for defending themselves against any threats to their pride and self-esteem that discontinuous organizational role changes so frequently provoke. These are very powerful motivational forces. Yet they are rarely discussed or acknowledged in the standard way that most companies manage an upward transition.

So what are organizations to do? Exhibit 2.1 (pages 32–33) lists several tactics and techniques that talent management, HR, and OD professionals and even senior managers can employ to help managers-in-transition overcome behavioral addiction and assist them through the processes of letting go and adding on.

Letting Go, Preserving, and Adding On

To find their way through any of the four career crossroads effectively, managers-in-transition must make conscious decisions to let go of some of their habitual or preferred lower-level perspectives, familiar responsibilities, and work habits. Discarding anachronistic work practices and routines will free them up so they can focus on the demands of the new responsibilities that they must master. This enables managers-in-transition to adapt to the novel demands of their higher-level roles. This process will be repeated each time managers-in-transition are confronted by the challenge of negotiating the next higher career shift or crossroad that they must navigate.

Prior to (or very soon after) navigating a crossroad, those who are most successful seem to recognize the need for and actively seek out ways to

Exhibit 2.1. Tactics and Techniques for Facilitating Upward Transitions

There are several things organizations can do to help managers-in-transition hit the ground running and successfully take charge of a more senior role. The table below contains a generic list of interventions for helping managers at all levels let go of irrelevant skills, perspectives, and values and add on new ones.

Letting Go	Adding On
Visible role models: Offer internal programs that include senior leaders in the firm who share their own journeys and discuss their own struggles with letting go of anachronistic skill sets—and the benefits they gained when they did let go.	*Integrated career planning and succession planning:* An underexploited synergy is the natural affinity career planning with individuals has with succession planning for the organization. Among other things, aligning these activities can provide managers with a realistic preview of what to expect in future roles and identify where targeted skills training may help.
Mentoring: Sponsor and encourage the development of mentoring relationships in which senior managers share their experiences of withdrawal and letting go with individuals on a similar career trajectory.	*Developmental assignments:* In anticipation of a transition, it may be advantageous to put the person on a task force or in a "stretch assignment" that requires, on a small scale, new skills that will be needed in the next role.

Letting Go	Adding On
Support groups: Provide a loosely structured forum where multiple managers-in-transition meet regularly to discuss how "what got them here won't keep them here." It is intended to facilitate the "grieving" of letting go as well as to provide encouragement and practical tips.	*Rotations:* Again as preparation for the next role, managers-in-transition can do a short stint in the functional units that they, if actually promoted, will be responsible for. This will expose them to the work, key people, and an inside perspective on a foreign topic.
Coaching with a psychologist: Managers-in-transition are unlikely to admit having difficulty; psychologically oriented coaches are uniquely suited to guide them through the emotional aspects of grieving and mourning in a confidential helping relationship.	*Action learning:* A bona fide action learning project (Marquardt, 1999), where ad hoc teams are presented with a novel business problem, is a powerful way to expose managers to alternative perspectives, take account of their biases and preferred ways of approaching problems, learn firsthand about essential interdependencies across the organization, and establish key relationships.

Note. As a general principle, all training and development and talent literature, materials, and intranet sites should communicate a consistent, clear, and succinct message about how positions on different levels require somewhat distinct skill sets. This will prepare upwardly mobile managers to expect change as they traverse the career pathways and crossroads.

develop proficiency in the new competencies and skill areas needed in the new role. For instance, in chapter 5 Martineau, Laskow, Moye, and Phillips describe how the Central Intelligence Agency is using competency models tailored for each level of management as a way of signaling to up-and-coming managers what will be needed in the next job. Such a road map is enormously helpful because managers-in-transition are on a journey that requires them to abandon the familiar and courageously enter new, unfamiliar territory— repeatedly. They must stay alert, be astute, and be cautious. To the naive, the new work and its demands may look deceptively familiar, particularly since managers-in-transition may feel insecure and understandably are motivated to deny any differences. Proactive inhibition (Coch & French, 1948), or what is more commonly known as shooting yourself in the foot, may amplify the difficulties that managers-in-transition may experience when trying to discard and let go of their habitual work patterns and practices. The keys to a successful transition at each career crossroad are letting go, preserving, and adding on (Freedman, 1995a, 1995b, 1998; Harrison, 1972). Figure 2.2 contains a graphic depiction of this triple challenge facing managers making an upward move.

Figure 2.2. The Tripartite Challenge of Transformational Change: Preserving, Letting Go, and Adding On

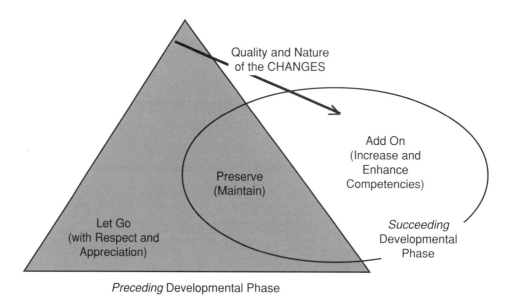

Letting Go

Managers-in-transition must stop doing or do less of some outmoded but familiar and comfortable responsibilities. They must let go of some of the competencies that led to success in their previous, lower-level jobs. Managers-in-transition probably felt confident in themselves and in their competencies; they felt comfortable when using these reliable competencies in those familiar contexts. They may have even become addicted to those familiar responsibilities and competencies because of the repeated success they brought. To let go of these reliable old friends, which may feel something like jumping off a nice safe raft into shark-infested waters, is easy to prescribe but difficult and threatening to do. Managers-in-transition need firm encouragement and support to fully experience (rather than deny) their personal behavioral addiction and cope with a withdrawal process, to grieve and mourn the loss of their emotional attachment to these familiar, comforting competencies.

Preserving

Managers-in-transition must preserve and continue to perform certain familiar responsibilities and apply preexisting competencies that have been, still are, and are likely to continue to be practical and useful. However, they will have to deal with a major conundrum: how will they accurately distinguish between those responsibilities and competencies of which they must let go and those that they must retain and preserve? Few people can make this distinction quickly and accurately. As in any trial-and-error process, errors in judgment are inevitable.

Adding On

Managers-in-transition must start or do more to quickly master and apply new, unprecedented, and discontinuous responsibilities and competencies. Managers-in-transition must adopt the role of learners. This can be uncomfortable unless they are high on what Lombardo and Eichinger (2000) call learning agility: constantly seeking and capitalizing on performance-enhancing developmental experiences. Many managers-in-transition experience the prospect of acquiring proficiency in applying new perspectives, information, concepts, strategies, methods, technologies, skills, and attitudes to be "awkward and embarrassing," as one such person described it. This only stands to reason: the learning curve is not an upward parabola—real-life learning curves start with a dip in performance as the individual struggles to acquire the basics and then begin the upward swoop as mastery takes place (Downey et al., 2001; Zaccaro & Banks, 2004). Managers-in-transition often expect their progress to be a straight, upward trend line. This expectation must be challenged. Upwardly mobile managers must understand that this parabolic curve is the normal pathway.

To protect themselves from the awkward feelings that accompany the initial dip in the real-life learning curve, some managers-in-transition may convince themselves that this is an unreasonable or unnecessary and inconvenient process. Often these are rationalizations that are intended to create a facade to contain their anxiety, which can be quite intense. Beneath their brittle bravado, most managers-in-transition harbor fundamental doubts about their own capacity to learn and to adapt (see Kaplan, 1999). They must learn that such self-doubt is natural and that they must harness and direct the energy generated by such feelings into constructive channels.

Applying the Model: The Special Case of Becoming the CEO

As they rise within large, complex organizations (which they thought they thoroughly understood), managers-in-transition inevitably discover, as they traverse each of the four career crossroads, that they are moving into quite different, very unfamiliar worlds. Like Dorothy, they might well say, "Toto, I don't think we're in Kansas anymore. . . ."

I have previously described (Freedman, 1998) the four critical career crossroads and the critical responsibilities and behaviors managers-in-transition must let go of, add on, and preserve to round out their repertoires. I have also described the critical prerequisite competencies and attributes the manager-in-transition needs to maneuver through each career crossroad. Readers interested in this thorough catalogue can find it in my 1998 article in *Consulting Psychology Journal*. In this chapter, for purposes of illustrating the demands of negotiating a career shift, I choose to focus on the most senior career crossroad: moving from executive manager of a portfolio of several businesses to the position of institutional leader, the chief executive officer (see crossroad 4 in figure 2.1).

The CEO Transition

This is the most visible career shift. Obviously, very few people are selected to serve in the role of an institutional leader. When this rare, singular event occurs, it usually has an extremely significant impact on the leader's former peers, the board of directors, the organization's external stakeholders (for example, customers, suppliers, competitors, regulatory agencies, the financial community, media, investors, and employees), and the organization's future. The installation of a new institutional leader usually signals that fundamental, systemwide changes will take place and that these changes will impact all parts, all levels, and relations with all stakeholders of an organization. The process for the selection of an institutional leader is often far more political than are lower-level promotions. Other than that, the selection criteria are quite similar to—and as soft as—those used to make staffing decisions at lower levels (see Sessa, Kaiser, Taylor, & Campbell, 1998).

One difference in top-level appointments is the sources that provide the candidates. The challenging question confronting most organizations is whether to grow or buy their future leaders. This is a widespread dilemma (see chapter 1 for recent benchmarking research). Most Western organizations seem to rely on executive recruiting firms to provide lists of prequalified candidates from which boards of directors can select senior leaders. Thus, they opt for buying rather than growing executives. This may be expedient, since most contemporary efforts to ensure organizational continuity by planning executive succession, managing intellectual executive capital, and providing executive development opportunities seem to be inadequate. My observation is that only a very small number of public, private, NGO, and nonprofit sector organizations seem willing to make sufficient investments in developing their internal executive talent so they can select their CEOs' successors from pools of fully qualified executive manager candidates.

The most critical and most common error made by boards of directors at this crossroad is assuming that new CEOs have very little to learn other than, perhaps, the core technologies of the organization. It can be self-defeating to assume that new institutional leaders need only continue to operate as they did as executive managers of a portfolio of several businesses or as CEOs of medium-sized companies. Like high blood pressure, it can be a silent killer to assume that new CEOs are simply adding a few new specialized businesses to their portfolios and that they do not need to unlearn any anachronistic practices or learn anything new about leading an organization in an uncertain environment.

Newly appointed CEOs should prepare themselves to experience a revolutionary change in self-concept and sense of identity. As institutional leaders, they must cope with the natural anxiety that comes from realizing that their ultimate value may be based on the quality of only a handful of extraordinarily consequential strategic decisions that they will make in any given year. The stakes are enormous and are matched by the pressure with which CEOs must learn to live. The job is exceedingly demanding and requires a nearly total dedication to the firm, often at the expense of work-life balance (Kaiser & Craig, 2004).

If they have been paying attention to their varied experiences as they worked their way through previous crossroads, they may have prepared themselves to learn how to unlearn and learn anew. If not previously, they will now have to learn how to climb a series of steep learning curves—often simultaneously, always quickly, and always substantively. Exhibit 2.2 lists some specific things that new CEOs will have to add on and let go of.

Implications of Skipping Crossroads

In my organization development and change consulting practice, I have encountered a number of situations in which CEOs have not traversed two or three of the career crossroads before being appointed to their current position. There are many justifications for such shortcuts. One might argue that the justifications are mostly rationalizations for hasty decision makers or politically motivated appointments. There is, however, the instance of an entrepreneurial innovator who illuminates several important implications of skipping or bypassing one or more lower-level career crossroads.

Rising within an established, stable organization is quite different from leading an organization at an earlier phase in its life cycle. For example, if and when they conclude that their companies are unwilling or unable to support the commercialization of their technological innovations, technologically gifted wunderkind are not unlikely to resign. Typically, such persons have been high-level individual contributors with little, if any, experience with the discontinuous challenges of traversing any of the career crossroads. Once in a while, one hears stories about these entrepreneurial innovators who leave their original employer but negotiate with their employer to take their patents with them to start up their own new technology-based ventures.

Whether they realize it or not, these courageous innovators are leaping from the first or second to the fourth career crossroad, omitting quite a bit of essential developmental experience. Theirs is a truly revolutionary challenge. These technologically driven, entrepreneurial leaders may be successful during the start-up and initial rapid growth phases of their new enterprises but are likely to be ineffective in leading them once they have achieved some degree of stability. Such unique individuals probably should bring in experienced managers to fill in the gaps in their capacities to fulfill the role of effective institutional leaders.

Exhibit 2.2. What New CEOs Must Let Go, Preserve, and Add On

Let Go (Stop or do less)	Preserve (Continue to do)	Add On (Start or do more)
Make quick, tactical, trade-off decisions.	Build and develop your subordinate executive managers into a high-performance team.	Serve as the most observable company figurehead interacting with the various internal and external corporate stakeholders.
Use a decisive and directive style that centers on your own judgment.	Serve as a mentor to promising subordinates (two or three levels down from you).	Establish and nurture relationships with external stakeholder groups and populations of constituents.
Collaborate with peers (you won't have any peers within your own organization now).	Recognize, reward, and publicize outstanding performance of individuals, teams, and subsystems.	Seek and develop mutually supportive affiliations with CEOs in other companies in your own and in other industries and with trade or professional associations.
Compete with peers (again, you won't have any peers, but whatever you do, you will have detractors).	Maintain and nurture strategic planning at corporate and divisional levels.	Articulate an attractive, compelling sense of corporate mission and purpose that employees and the investment community can identify with.

(continued)

Exhibit 2.2. What New CEOs Must Let Go, Preserve, and Add On (cont.)

Let Go (Stop or do less)	Preserve (Continue to do)	Add On (Start or do more)
Expect that you can have a great family life in addition to a highly successful career as a CEO. You may have to sacrifice a balance between your career and your personal and family life.	Identify and challenge limiting organizational beliefs to ensure their relevance or discard and replace them.	Enhance the capacity to deal with ambiguity and complexity in a system of unprecedented scope and scale.
Build up your personal facade or image.	Maintain a global perspective.	Apply a systems view to understand complexity, interdependency, the nature of alignment, and a comfort with ambiguity.
	Experiment and take reasonable risks.	Recruit, empower, and support your subordinate executive managers.
	Do the right things.	Nurture or start a formal executive succession system (not just an emergency program).
		Consider what legacy you want to leave to the company after you retire or depart.

Alas, they rarely do what they probably should do. It may be difficult for them to understand and accept the need to supplement themselves since to do so would mean they would have to acknowledge their own personal limitations or shortcomings, which is difficult for driven high achievers. Those who fail to compensate for their limitations may be forced out by, for example, the venture capitalists and other investors who funded their start-up companies and now want to see a reliable flow of profits. Some entrepreneurial innovators may not be temperamentally suitable to make the shift to leading an organization once it reaches maturity. Such persons may have to let go of their creation and consider moving on to start up another in what may become a series of innovative enterprises. Or they may rescue themselves, take a role like the chief innovation officer, and turn the leadership of the new venture over to someone with the requisite experience, competencies, and temperament to lead the enterprise into the future.

Conclusion

When we observe an under-performing or dysfunctional leader or manager, it serves no constructive purpose to castigate that individual. Rather, we must keep in mind the possibility of organizational collusion. With necessary and sufficient preparation of individuals plus organizational support and effective performance management, we might identify and do something useful with under-performing leaders. However, ideal organizational conditions rarely prevail. Frequently, what looks like a dysfunctional leader is merely a product of prevailing organizational conditions. Therefore, rather than blaming the victim, it seems more practical to examine the organization and its executive development and succession systems to determine how to ensure that the behavior of managers-in-transition will enable them to take the leadership roles and apply the proper competencies to the relevant challenges in ways that contribute to the realization of the organizations' vision, mission, goals, strategies, and values.

Organizational conditions can exacerbate or ameliorate flawed individual behavior. It is enlightening to illuminate and specify those organizational assumptions and practices that help and hinder effective executive leadership. The results of such an exercise can establish practical diagnostic criteria that could enable managers-in-transition and their consultants to identify areas for supportive, corrective, or preventive intervention.

Notes

1. The term *business* is in quotes because this crossroad is intended to cover any complete business process composed of a sequence of value-adding but discrete functions in public sector, NGO, and nonprofit organizations in addition to those in the private, for-profit sector.

2. It is also important to note that managers should not remain on the same pathway, or in the same type of role, for more than three or four years. Beyond that, people become too "addicted" to using familiar routines that may have been success-ful at lower levels as they try to adapt and respond to the new demands presented by crossing the next career crossroad.

References

Charan, R., Drotter, S., & Noel, J. (2001). *The leadership pipeline: How to build the leadership-powered company.* San Francisco: Jossey-Bass.

Coch, L., & French, J. (1948). Overcoming resistance to change. *Human Relations, 1,* 512–532.

Downey, D., March, T., & Berkman, A. (2001). *Assimilating new leaders: The key to executive retention.* New York: AMACOM.

Freedman, A. M. (1995a). *Executive succession planning in relation to strategic planning and human resource development.* Invited keynote address, Human Resource and Development Conference, Anchorage, AK.

Freedman, A. M. (1995b). Stress management training. In W. M. Tracey (Ed.), *Human resources management and development handbook* (2nd ed., pp. 1063–1077). New York: AMACOM.

Freedman, A. M. (1998). Pathways and crossroads to institutional leadership. *Consulting Psychology Journal, 50,* 131–151.

Gabarro, J. J. (1987). *The dynamics of taking charge.* Boston: Harvard Business School Press.

Harrison, R. (1972). Role negotiations: A tough-minded approach to team develop-ment. In W. W. Burke & H. A. Hornstein (Eds.), *The social technology of organi-zation development* (pp. 84–96). La Jolla, CA: University Associates.

Kaiser, R. B., & Craig, S. B. (2004, April). What gets you there won't keep you there: Managerial behaviors related to effectiveness at the bottom, middle, and top. In R. B. Kaiser & S. B. Craig (Cochairs), *Filling the pipe I: Studying man-agement development across the hierarchy.* Symposium presented at the Nineteenth Annual Conference of the Society for Industrial and Organizational Psychology, Chicago.

Kaplan, R. E. (1999). *Internalizing strengths: An overlooked way of overcoming weaknesses in managers.* Greensboro, NC: Center for Creative Leadership.

Kaplan, R. E., & Kaiser, R. B. (2003). Developing versatile leadership. *MIT Sloan Management Review, 44*(4), 19–26.

Lombardo, M. M., & Eichinger, R. W. (2000). High potentials as high learners. *Human Resource Management, 39,* 321–330.

Mahler, W. R., & Wrightnour, W. F. (1973). *Executive continuity: How to build and retain an effective management team.* Homewood, IL: Dow Jones-Irwin.

Marquardt, M. J. (1999). *Action learning in action.* Palo Alto, CA: Davies-Black Publishing.

McCall, M. W., Jr., Lombardo, M. M., & Morrison, A. M. (1988). *The lessons of experience: How successful executives develop on the job.* Lexington, MA: Lexington Books.

Mintzberg, H. (1994). Rounding out the manager's job. *Sloan Management Review, 36*(1), 11–26.

Sessa, V. I., Kaiser, R., Taylor, J. K., & Campbell, R. J. (1998). *Executive selection: A research report on what works and what doesn't.* Greensboro, NC: Center for Creative Leadership.

Zaccaro, S. J. (2001). *The nature of executive leadership: A conceptual and empirical analysis of success.* Washington, DC: American Psychological Association.

Zaccaro, S. J., & Banks, D. (2004, April). Developmental work assignments for middle and upper level organizational leaders. In R. B. Kaiser & S. B. Craig (Cochairs), *Filling the pipe I: Studying management development across the hierarchy.* Symposium presented at the Nineteenth Annual Conference of the Society for Industrial and Organizational Psychology, Chicago.

The Challenges of General Manager Transitions

Amy Kates and Diane Downey
Downey Kates Associates

There may be nothing more important to an organization's succession efforts than building a strong cadre of general managers. Yet making the transition to the general manager role is fraught with difficulty. It is at this point where many successful careers derail (McCall & Lombardo, 1983; Shipper & Dillard, 2000). According to the Corporate Leadership Council, turnover among newly hired executives within the first three years of taking a new job is as high as 50 percent (as cited in Sweeney, 1999). In chapter 2 Arthur Freedman explains myriad psychological challenges involved in managerial promotions. We will use the pathways-and-crossroads framework he describes as well as introduce some additional considerations to enrich the model. Whereas Freedman describes how to apply the framework to transitions to the CEO level, we focus on the transition to the general manager role.

We define the general manager position as involving broad, overall responsibility for a line of business or set of functions. It is the first level of management where managers have to lead other managers without firsthand knowledge of their disciplines. In many organizations, it is the first step into the executive ranks from middle management. For every CEO transition, there are dozens of transitions at this level. And the importance of these general manager transitions is obvious: one of them is likely to be tomorrow's CEO.

Take the case of Phil, a brilliant aerospace engineer at a client organization. In just fifteen years after graduate school he had been rapidly promoted up through the technical ranks until he was a head of engineering at a large defense contractor. Two years ago he was promoted from a functional manager to vice president in charge of a new product line. But Phil was unable to make the leap from being a functional manager to a cross-functional leader at the general manager level. The product launch was a failure, and Phil's credibility in the company suffered. Within eighteen months, he had left to go back to an engineering job at a smaller company. The shame of it was that Phil's general manager career at the defense contractor didn't have to wind up as another derailment case. For one thing, he wasn't adequately prepared for the major transition. Further, he didn't have much support from his new boss, HR, his team, a mentor, or even an outside coach as he made the move. And with a vague sense of what he had to let go of and add on to make the leap, he wasn't fully sure he even wanted the increase in scope and scale.

In this chapter, we delve into the specific case of new general managers, with a particular focus on what the organization (that is, hiring managers, HR, and talent management staff) can do to support them and maximize the success rate of these key managerial moves. We highlight some ways that managing the transition is different for those promoted from within and external hires. Throughout, we draw upon examples and share lessons learned from organizations we've studied and consulted with on the design and execution of general manager transition plans over the last ten years.

The Value of General Managers

General managers are the lifeblood of any business. Up to this point in their careers, managers are often "manager-producers." They are promoted because of their technical knowledge and because they can coach and guide subordinates in the execution of their work. Functional managers can troubleshoot and solve problems as they arise, since they have often faced similar issues themselves in the past.

The general manager role is decidedly different. When placed in this role for the first time, managers are responsible for work they may have no expertise in, or even little appreciation for. For instance, in her role as director of marketing, our client Celeste had been frequently frustrated by the finance unit at budget time. She always felt they were too conservative and didn't understand how marketing drove the dynamics of the business. When Celeste was promoted to lead the business, the finance director began reporting to her. Celeste noted after her first year as a general manager that one of her biggest struggles was not only understanding enough about finance to make good decisions but also letting go of her old attitudes and appreciating the value and perspective that the unit brought.

It is precisely this ability to manage the unknown that distinguishes the general manager role and makes it so valuable to an organization. When you can no longer fall back on functional expertise, you must rely on the true management and influence skills of working through people and processes to make good decisions, implement change, and get results. Competencies such as assessing and hiring the right talent, setting up monitoring and feedback systems, and building a high-performing team become more important than any in-depth technical knowledge that you bring to the position (for more on unique executive competencies, see chapter 5).

When an organization's leaders know they have a set of general managers who can fill a variety of positions, they have real "bench strength." With bench strength, the organization is much better positioned to grow through acquisition, by launching new lines of business, or by reaching into new markets. The deliberate development and rotation of general managers is one of the most effective ways to transfer skills, best practices, and desired cultural norms across a dispersed and complex company. And of course, general managers are the primary source for senior executive talent.

Drying Up of the Management Pipeline

Too many companies find their pipeline drying up at the general manager level and discover that they need to hire from outside to fill gaps at higher levels. Ram Charan (2005) has noted that because of a lack of programs dedicated to grooming managers for top positions, 37 percent of Fortune 1000 companies are run by external recruits. He cites a Corporate Leadership Council survey that found that almost half of companies who had hired members of their executive teams from outside reported that they did so because developing internal candidates would be either too expensive or too time-consuming. At the same time, overall demographic trends indicate that the demand for experienced managers and executives will become only more intense in the coming decades. In the United States, the demographic dip that followed the baby boom has resulted in a shortage of workers in their thirties and early forties, the time when people are typically ready to make the turn to general manager. (The baby bust, or Generation X, is generally considered to be made up of people born from 1965 to 1975.) In the 1990s, the number of workers between the ages of twenty-five and thirty-four declined by 14 percent (Watson Wyatt, 2003). According to a study by the Bureau of Labor Statistics, when workers from the baby boom generation begin to retire in the United States, it will create a gap of about 10 million more jobs than there will be workers to fill them (as cited in Frank, Finnegan, & Taylor, 2004).

At the same time, other studies indicate that older workers are likely to retire later in the coming decade to make up for stock market losses and the shift from defined benefit pensions (that guarantee a retirement income) to defined contribution retirement plans (that are dependent on personal saving rates and the vagaries of the market). An AARP study shows that more than 63 percent of workers over fifty plan to work at least part-time in retirement. However, only 10 percent expect to be working full-time at the same type of work that they are currently engaged in (Brown, 2003). Therefore, while there may be more older workers than ever in the workforce, we can expect that few will be in the same type of demanding management roles they now occupy. In fact, the same study reports that over half of those surveyed plan to work for enjoyment, not money. This gap will be felt especially acutely at the higher levels of organizations as the leadership pipeline begins to run dry.

The General Manager Career Turn

Making the turn to general manager represents a substantial step up in leadership and accountability. One primary difference from the functional manager role is that the general manager typically has full end-to-end accountability for a good portion of the business, along with profit and loss (P&L) responsibility. For example, at one of our clients, general managers were each responsible for sales, marketing, and product development for their line of business, with full P&L responsibility. Finance and other support functions were managed by peers. In that same firm, however, we also considered the director of operations to be a general manager, even though he did not have P&L responsibility. He managed a disparate set of functions, including manufacturing plants and refineries, customer service, logistics, and purchasing. The defining characteristic of the general manager role is oversight of multiple, unrelated functional units.

The pathways-and-crossroads model presents a useful way of conceptualizing management advancement, particularly reflecting how general manager roles differ from roles at other levels (see figure 3.1). The crossroads are a series of turns, with each turn representing a discontinuous change in responsibility. Each crossroad (or turn) requires a different set of skills, work values, use of time, and time perspective (Charan, Drotter, & Noel, 2001; Freedman, 1998). The turn to the general manager role—going from managing a function to managing a business—is particularly demanding, since it represents the first move away from the particular skill area in which most managers have formal education and training as well as on-the-job experience.

**Figure 3.1. Locating the General Manager Transition:
The Pathways-and-Crossroads Model**

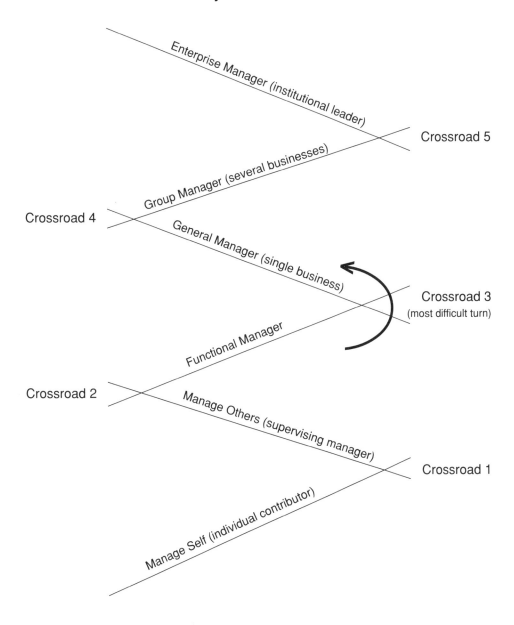

Note. This version of the pathways-and-crossroads model differs slightly from the version used in chapter 2. We have added "functional manager" to clarify the intermediate steps between supervisor and general manager (see Charan et al., 2001).

Letting Go and Adding On

As with all transitions, successfully making the leap requires new general managers to let go of or quit using skills and values that were important to their success in their previous roles but are inappropriate for their new roles. It also requires them to add on new skills and preserve or modify existing skills and competencies (Freedman, 1998; see also chapter 2 and exhibit 3.1). In particular, there are three key learning areas that new general managers must address. First is a working knowledge of the different functional areas under their supervision. New general managers have to learn enough about every function within their groups—even those they have no experience in and little technical knowledge of, and perhaps even place little value on—to make decisions and trade-offs and integrate the operations of these diverse functions within a single coherent and viable business strategy. Second, the transition also entails a shift in a manager's time horizon, away from focusing on the relatively short-term goals of a functional group to the medium- and long-term strategic goals of a business. Finally, and perhaps most difficult, it necessitates a shift in mind-set from a practical, functional perspective— "Can we do it?"—to a strategic enterprise perspective—"Should we do this? Is it profitable?"

Key Challenges of the General Manager Transition

An array of complicating factors makes the transition to general manager uniquely difficult. In the first two management career turns, to supervising manager and to functional manager, people are assumed to be working in the same business or function. They may have a broader scope of responsibility, but their work likely has many of the same dimensions. While all turns in the pathways-and-crossroads model present challenges, it is this third crossroad, from functional manager to general manager, that may present the greatest degree of change for new executives. They need to establish credibility with new teams, made up of people who believe they know more about their work than the executive does, and who are probably right. Appropriate mentors and role models are scarce, since there are fewer general managers than functional managers in an organization. Previous incumbents in the role may not have succeeded or may be gone, or the business may have been reconfigured. As one of our clients noted, "When I became fully accountable for the business in two countries, there was nobody I could go to next door and say, 'Hey, I've

---

Exhibit 3.1. Letting Go and Adding On for New General Managers

In addition to preserving and building the skills to assess and hire the right talent, set up monitoring and feedback systems, and build a high-performing team, new general managers need to let go of some behaviors and skills that may have served them well in the past and add on some new ones.

Let Go	Add On
Building depth of one's own technical expertise	Working knowledge of new functional areas beyond area of training and expertise
Narrow, practical, functional perspective	Broad, enterprise, strategic view
Short-term—"Can we do it?"—functional strategies	Longer term—"Will it be profitable?"—business strategies
Hands-on troubleshooting and problem solving	Trust, coaching others through crises
Competitive attitudes toward peer functions	Appreciation for the contributions of each area of the business
Minimizing conflict within the team, emphasizing harmony and consensus	Valuing diverse organizational viewpoints, new skills to surface differences and constructively manage tension

---

got this problem. What do you think I should do about it?' I mean, if I called somebody, that person may have had more experience than I, but, of course, not in that same position or at that point in time."

The irony is that high performers moving into general manager roles often receive the least organizational support in the form of a transition plan, facilitated sessions with their new bosses, experienced mentors to help along the way, or systematic feedback to gauge how things are going. The assumption is "You've been promoted because you were successful. So keep on being successful!" It is a questionable article of faith to assume continued success, since the expectations and requirements in the new job are radically different from anything the talented manager has experienced in the past. This raises a natural question: what can be done to help new general managers hit the ground running and meet these expectations?

Each person's transition to a new managerial role is shaped by a unique set of factors: the individual's skills and experience, the organizational culture, the health of the assumed business, the inherited talent, and the performance expectations. However, we have seen several common and predictable challenges in our experience working with dozens of organizations and hundreds of their managers and from in-depth interviews with the people charged with creating internal systems to support the success of new leaders. Exhibit 3.2 discusses six prominent challenges confronting new general managers.

Navigating Unfamiliar Waters: Learning the Culture and Expectations

Much individual assimilation work appropriately focuses on helping new leaders build networks and relationships and quickly understand the political landscape and inner workings of the organization. This typically occurs in the first month or two, to get new leaders on their feet and provide a window of opportunity to hold exploratory meetings and ask questions about the basics. For most general managers, this window closes quickly. The honeymoon period of assessing the situation, listening, and learning soon comes to an end, and action is expected.

Some organizations are implementing mechanisms that acknowledge that the learning curve in a complex business is much longer than a few months. A large industrial engineering firm has developed a course for general managers who have been in the role for three to nine months. The program is focused on systems and processes and includes a decision-making simulation mirroring the multifaceted nature of the business. It is designed specifically to allow these managers to ask in-depth questions after they've had real experience on the job. Even the existence of the course itself communicates the message that it is okay to still be asking questions six months in.

Such a program is fairly easy to implement and can be as simple as a daylong seminar held once or twice a year. Start with a survey of what new general managers want to know and where they feel less confident. Bring in

Exhibit 3.2. Challenges and Strategies for General Manager Turns	
Challenge	**Strategy**
Navigating Unfamiliar Waters: Learning the Culture and Expectations	Particularly for internal promotions, the gap in understanding how to operate in the new role is often underestimated. Smart companies help the new general manager make the connections and learn the ropes.
Coping with Increased Complexity: Creating Business Strategies	General manager roles often entail an exponential leap in complexity, and new general managers are likely to be uncomfortable asking for help. Support the new leader in developing a business strategy and involving others in decision making.
Managing Former Peers: Letting Go and Assuming Command	The toughest situation is being promoted to manage former colleagues. Use lots of feedback to uncover concerns early and build the general manager's credibility with a skeptical audience.
Building a Leadership Team: Executing through Others	The quality of the general manager's direct reports is critical to his or her success. Help with the talent assessment, balance skill gaps in the leader with strength on the team, and create an appreciation for candor, conflict, and debate in meetings.
Establishing a Personal Leadership Brand: Preparing for Increased Visibility	The move to general manager is a move into corporate leadership. The increased visibility requires increased attention to words and actions. Help manage first impressions and create a positive executive presence.
Transferring Knowledge: Preserving the Institutional Memory	A new general manager frequently means someone else is leaving, retiring, or moving on in the company. Use the transition to transfer vital knowledge to the new leader and preserve institutional memory.

senior leaders to cover these topics. More important, design the day to encourage a lot of interaction and discussion. Use a good facilitator who will create a safe environment for people to raise questions. An added bonus from such a program is that it helps to create networks and relationships among your future leaders from different parts of the organization.

In 2003, Wal-Mart International instituted what it calls the Next Leader program. New external general manager hires spend up to six months in a complete learning and listening mode. They are exposed to all facets of the company and are free to attend key meetings and conduct informational interviews, free from formal job responsibilities. They are not expected to deliver any results or get involved in any specific project. Rather, they are to immerse themselves in the company's culture and strategy. After six months they are placed in a senior-level international assignment, allowing them to stretch and apply their experiences and learning to the business. Wal-Mart has found the program to be a worthwhile investment to ensure that external executive hires can successfully navigate the specific culture and management practices of the company. Interestingly, they have found that executive hires from other retail companies sometimes have a higher recalibration curve than those without a retail background. They often need longer in the program to embrace Wal-Mart's management and business practices. As much as the program is used to communicate the unique Wal-Mart philosophy, it is also used to help new hires understand which of the behaviors and approaches that made them successful in the past potentially may not work in their new roles at the company.

These new Next Leaders at Wal-Mart are also encouraged to partner with someone in the company who has recently gone through a similar transition experience. While HR facilitates these contacts, it does not make the matches. Finding an appropriate buddy to learn from in this circumstance is a highly personalized process and depends on the two people forming a personal relationship. Parallel to previous findings from research on mentoring (for example, Kram, 1985), Wal-Mart has found that overformalizing the buddy system did not offer the full benefits for either associate.

At American Express, each new general manager creates a "Learning Plan" that includes areas of business knowledge and skill focus, organizational and local culture issues, an employee communication strategy, and a personal development plan. The indoctrination into the organization's culture is the most important part for outside hires. It focuses on how work gets done outside formal systems, how decisions are made, and how to effectively introduce and sell new ideas. External hires are provided with a coach and full 360-degree feedback at the four-month mark to determine what course corrections need to be made. For internal promotions, transition coaching is available and focuses on anticipating issues and planning ahead.

Coping with Increased Complexity: Creating Business Strategies

The move to general manager often represents a quantum leap in scope and complexity, no matter how demanding one's prior functional position was. It requires managers to take a broader view and to ask a new set of questions. Rather than focusing on how the work will get done, the questions that keep general managers up at night are "Is this the right business model? Will it be profitable?" Previously, the managers may have set functional strategy or worked as part of a leadership team that was engaged in forming the business strategy. Now they are responsible for leading strategy development, selling it upward to managers and laterally to peers, and then gaining alignment and support within their own teams.

This is the place where new general managers often stumble, for a number of reasons. The focus on leadership over the past decade has made companies aware of the danger of promoting the best technical performers into leadership positions. As a result, organizations have a heightened awareness of the importance of generic leadership qualities (see chapter 4). At the same time, the relentless emphasis on short-term results often leads to the promotion of problem solvers, not integrators. For example, a senior manager at one of our client organizations was a finance director when he was selected to head a new business after the acquisition of a competitor. "Greg" was known as a firefighter; his style was all about solving today's problems. He was admired for his practical, cut-to-the-chase approach, and he swiftly set about making integration and system conversion decisions. However, formulating long-term strategies to grow the business was not where his heart was. And where there is a lack of interest, you can safely bet on finding a lack of skill. Nine months into his new role, Greg had made significant cost cuts but had taken no action on a growth strategy.

At the general manager level, the increase in data and information can easily lead to overload. Those who are able to take a holistic view, synthesize disparate data to identify trends, and sort out what is important tend to have an easier time shifting to a strategic mind-set. Successful general managers have strong business acumen and understand the dynamics of the business without getting bogged down in operational details. Of course, no matter how much natural talent or interest one may have in setting strategy, lack of experience makes it unlikely that these talents will have been sharply honed prior to promotion to the general manager level.

Another barrier is that people who have moved into general manager roles often don't want to admit that they are uncomfortable devising business strategies or that they just don't know how. They think they have to do it alone and fear that asking for help will be perceived as a sign of weakness. The process of moving from being new in a role (whether promoted from within or hired from the outside) to being a successful, effective, comfortable leader follows two separate paths: intellectual and emotional (Downey, March, & Berkman, 2001). The intellectual experience is the fairly smooth learning curve representing knowledge about the new company and job and how to get the work done. When we plot the emotional experience, however, it is more of a roller coaster. It can take as long as eighteen months for someone to gain the confidence that comes with competence in a new role (see figure 3.2).

Figure 3.2. The Intellectual and Emotional Elements of Assimilation

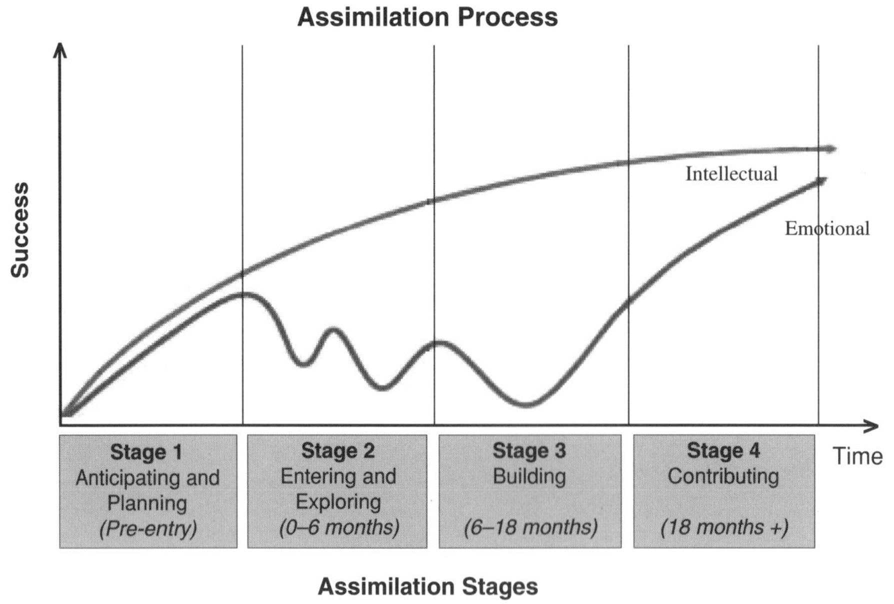

Assimilation Process

Stage 1	Stage 2	Stage 3	Stage 4
Anticipating and Planning	Entering and Exploring	Building	Contributing
(Pre-entry)	*(0–6 months)*	*(6–18 months)*	*(18 months +)*

Assimilation Stages

Note. This portrayal of the different trajectories for the development of intellectual and emotional success in managerial transitions is based on *Assimilating New Leaders: The Key to Executive Retention* (Downey et al., 2001). The stages of assimilation, a concept not used in this chapter, are fully elaborated and explained in that book.

There are several implications of this phenomenon for both HR managers and new general managers. The first is the importance of not expecting emotional comfort to keep up with the pace of intellectual achievements. Because of this difference in pace, the assimilation process is often more difficult than most people expect, even for experienced executives. As new general managers learn more about how the organization operates and the expectations for them in their new roles, they experience continued and growing success. Emotionally, however, new leaders are often confronted by unexpected resistance or barriers at the cultural level that are a result of events and values from the organization's past, of which they may not be aware. These "cultural potholes" often carry an emotional charge that is out of proportion to the logic of the situation. Preparing new general managers for these events and addressing them directly when they occur can help to even out the emotional learning curve. The organization can help a new leader deal with these barriers by raising awareness of the difficulties new leaders face and providing a supportive atmosphere that will not interpret the normal emotional fluctuations of the assimilation process as managerial or strategic incompetence.

Making the transition to leading with a strategic view of the entire business, instead of only one's own area of functional expertise, is one of the most difficult shifts to make, both in intellectual and emotional terms. The ability to think strategically shows up on nearly every company's leadership competency model (see chapter 5). But the difference between creating a strategy for a single functional unit and creating a fully coordinated, cross-functional business strategy is rarely delineated. There are a number of practices you can employ to support new executives with this aspect of the transition.

One is to assess for this competency in the hiring and promotion processes. Skill at execution is relatively easy to determine, but if creating and implementing a strategy will be important to the new role, it should be built into the assessment process as well. Involve the hiring managers (that is, the general manager's new set of bosses) in defining what they expect to see. Probe to understand not just the candidate's skill but also his or her motivation and style. The reason for shortcomings in strategic thinking may be lack of experience or, for people like Greg, a dislike for that part of the job. If this gap is not uncovered early, it can derail a career and a business.

Another action that HR and internal talent managers can take is to make it acceptable, and even positive, to ask for help. New general managers may overrate their own abilities or not want to appear inadequate. As part of the transition support program, it should be made clear that strategy development is an important, albeit understandably unfamiliar, part of the role, and help should be proactively provided to assist in this work. Create an expectation that the general manager will enlist others in this role. For example, after seeing Greg stall in his efforts to create a strategy for the integrated business, his HR partner and his manager encouraged him to hold a facilitated two-day strategy-planning meeting off-site with his top thirty-five team members. Hearing the group talk about where the business needed to go and the potential opportunities and options made the business prospects real to Greg. It turned an abstract concept into an exciting and more tangible object that he was able to grasp. He also saw the value of participation and the credit he received for involving his people instead of the ridicule he feared for failing to be a more adept strategic thinker. The process helped him make the mental shift from being a functional manager whose personal involvement in the work is vital to becoming a general manager whose primary role is orchestrating how the work will get done. He was able to take the output from the meeting and enlist his senior team to build and rally around a successful growth plan.

Wal-Mart's approach to general manager development places heavy emphasis on learning from experience, perhaps the single greatest source of leadership development (McCall, Lombardo, & Morrison, 1988). High potentials preparing for general manager roles are given opportunities to learn and grow through a succession of increasingly complex stretch assignments. The company has learned the hard way that it is much more than an increase in scope to go from managing twenty stores to managing five hundred stores. There is an exponential increase in complexity. Now new general managers may start with twenty stores, then move to another country to manage the same number, and then move to a position with more stores in a third country. Wal-Mart talent managers have learned to pace development so that individual capacity and capability grow along with the complexity of the job. Moves for high potentials are carefully planned and sequenced—as much as market change, family situations, and individual interest allow—to expose the manager to the right set of developmental experiences. For each move, the individual's strategic ability is matched as well as possible to the current need to ensure there is growth and learning along with business success.

Managing Former Peers: Letting Go and Assuming Command

General managers promoted from within face a unique set of challenges. Several former peers were likely also under consideration for the top spot, and the promoted manager may be inheriting bruised feelings and resentment. Even when the individual is respected, there may be sour grapes. This can raise skepticism about the person's readiness to take on the job, or suspicions may arise about the political nature of decisions.

A widely used technique to establish credibility and ensure that the new manager is on the right track is formalized feedback gathered four to eight weeks after the person has assumed the new role. In some organizations this is done by an external coach, but frequently it is collected by a senior HR partner or internal talent management specialist. Direct reports are interviewed to determine what is working about the leader's style, actions, and behaviors and what he or she should continue; where there are concerns and what he or she needs to do less of or stop doing; and what the primary challenges are for the coming year. The coach identifies trends in the feedback and delivers it to the manager, and together they pick the few items that, if addressed, would have the greatest impact on the performance of the team.

Common feedback for new general managers is to stop micromanaging, particularly in the functional area from which the manager was promoted. Old habits die hard. Letting go of the work that so recently provided satisfaction and self-worth while focusing on new tasks, many of which are much more amorphous, difficult to execute, and sometimes simply foreign, is often a challenge (Freedman, 1998; see also chapter 2). Unfortunately, natural uncertainty and insecurity during the first months or year of the transition can provoke behaviors in the new leader that subordinates perceive as a lack of trust in the team and overinvolvement in their work.

One way to address this is for HR and the hiring manager to ensure that a strong replacement is selected to fill the position left by the promoted manager. Too often the general manager's new boss may believe that because of the general manager's technical expertise, weakness can be tolerated in that area. As a result, if the replacement hired at the functional level is weak, a new general manager ends up de facto managing his or her old function along with the new responsibilities. This creates an impossible set of expectations and results in a job that is simply too large.

Another way to help new managers let go and build trust with the team is to help them think through how they will monitor the work and the business: what reports and data will they need for decision making? What do they need to know to be sufficiently informed for discussions that take place on the leadership team they are now part of (that is, their boss's team)? Simply being explicit in initial discussions with new subordinates about data needs and how that information will be used can eliminate much of the misunderstanding and frustration that subordinates often feel around the seemingly random requests for reports.

A telltale indication that a general manager transition is on track is whether employees are initiating asking for help or are waiting for the new leader to tell them what to do. This is the time when momentum can be easily lost—especially for internal promotions. At one large North American insurance company, new general managers are provided with extra coaching on how to assume leadership of a group that is composed of their former peers. This firm has found that it is important for the managers to establish and communicate early on what is going to change, what will stay the same, and what the group needs to know about their leadership styles. The goal is to reduce uncertainty and the loss of productivity that it often brings.

This company also places emphasis on managing first impressions during initial staff meetings with the new team. HR even gets involved in proactively managing the "rumor mill." Within the first few weeks of an appointment, HR will meet with the new general manager's direct reports to identify their concerns, help them understand his or her style, and reinforce the reasons behind the hiring decision. They have found that this serves to build a more positive view as these direct reports talk to their own staffs and peers in other divisions. It helps give the new manager the benefit of the doubt among a skeptical audience.

The hiring manager can also be instrumental in easing the way for the new manager to assume leadership of former peers. At American Express, part of the assimilation process is coaching the new general manager's boss on how to best support the new manager. HR staff reminds the boss of the importance of frequently revisiting goals and objectives and giving feedback. Since HR is cognizant of the demands on these executives, this is provided in the form of "three quick, easy things you can do" rather than an overly burdensome process.

Building a Leadership Team: Executing through Others

Building an effective team is a key responsibility of leaders at all organizational levels. For new general managers, however, building and maintaining a strong leadership team is different from team building at lower levels. Because of their own technical knowledge gaps, new general managers have to have complete confidence in the capabilities of each team member. There are several issues to anticipate in this area.

First, there may be discomfort in assessing the performance of former peers. It is likely they had an arm's-length relationship based on the tacit understanding that "We both sit on the leadership team, but if you stay out of my business, I'll stay out of yours." In addition, new leaders may be inexperienced in assessing other functional areas or more comfortable doing a technical assessment, rather than a managerial talent assessment. In addition, even if one is proficient at assessing the capabilities of others, it takes a lot of skill and self-awareness to identify one's own weak spots (in skills, perspective, or experience) and identify how others can compensate for those gaps.

New leaders also need to develop an appreciation for contention on their leadership team. Multifunctional teams are intended to elicit different points of view. Often new general managers have to hold back from pushing for consensus and compromise for the sake of harmony. Rather, they may need to learn new skills to surface issues and harness the varying perspectives to reach better decisions.

Many executive coaches don't work with teams, and the limitations of a coaching approach that is purely focused at the individual level can manifest themselves at this point. It can yield tremendous dividends for a new general manager to have an internal or external coach who can help with the assessment of talent on the team, is comfortable with team dynamics, and can even facilitate some of the first meetings.

As important as it is to help new general managers make good decisions about the composition of their new teams, it is also sometimes necessary to hold the new manager back from making personnel changes too quickly (see Gabarro, 1987). Managers can feel that making changes or bringing in new people is essential to establishing command and credibility, but these almost predictable reshufflings contribute to the distraction and disruption felt by frontline employees. Unless it is a turnaround situation in which the team has already been determined to be part of the problem, managers should be urged to take time to assess their personnel and hold off on making changes.

Establishing a Personal Leadership Brand: Preparing for Increased Visibility

The promotion to general manager is characterized by a higher level of visibility in the company. Even if it is an internal promotion, it is frequently the turn when the person goes from knowing a fair number of people in his or her organization to feeling that "they all know me and I hardly know anyone." In their communications, general managers address a much more diverse audience than before, an audience that often speaks a different organizational language. Informality may no longer be appropriate, and presentations should not contain the jargon, technical terms, or insider references that worked with a purely functional audience. A different level of executive presence is required.

Linda Reese, a partner at the consulting firm Executive OnBoarding, has worked with many organizations to set up transition support systems. She puts an emphasis on helping the new leader establish a "leadership brand strategy." Early assessment includes a focus on what is positive about the person's style and what might possibly diminish the person's effectiveness. Specific coaching strategies are put in place to help the leader project the confidence appropriate for the new role and to achieve a balance between his or her genuine personal style and the expectations and role requirements of the more senior position.

At the insurance company referred to above, the HR function has found that in addition to coaching the new general manager, there is often a need to educate the broader employee population about what general managers do. Key messages about what to expect in this role are embedded into the town hall presentations—dubbed Leader Forums—that new general managers are expected to hold with their employees. These messages include the company's expectation that its senior leaders, including general managers, will focus on building talent, teams, and relationships and the "why" of the work. The "how to" has been pushed to lower levels of managers and supervisors.

Transferring Knowledge: Preserving the Institutional Memory

A frequently overlooked challenge is the transfer of knowledge from the outgoing leader to the new general manager. Valuable information regarding the history of the business, the rationale and results of past decisions, the quality of the team, and key linkages and pitfalls may be lost when there is no opportunity to meet with the person who last held the job. Of course, if the previous manager failed, this information may not be reliable. And with the rapid pace of reorganizations, the new leader may be stepping into a newly created role for which there is no precedent. But most often an opening is the result of a reshuffling of the management ranks, and there is an opportunity for the two managers to connect and share knowledge.

With the looming retirement of so many senior managers over the next decade and the potential loss of their collective institutional memory, organizations are becoming more aware of the need to capture these insights. American Express encourages a new manager to speak with the person who previously held the position, but it is also wrestling with the larger challenge of retaining these forms of organizational and intellectual capital that are so hard to document.

Many of our clients and associates report that this is an effort that is unlikely to happen if left to chance and the initiative of the incoming leader. On the other hand, they have found that relatively small interventions that legitimize the conversation and provide some structure go a long way toward helping new general managers mine the knowledge of the people they are replacing.

At Pfizer, many HR partners encourage such meetings to take place, when possible and appropriate. The discussion focuses on insights and lessons learned. It is particularly encouraged for international assignments when a local functional manager is moving into a country manager position and there is a need to transfer corporate knowledge from the incumbent. These meetings are also encouraged when general managers are moving from smaller to larger countries and need guidance on local culture and business practices. Pfizer is also beginning to focus on becoming more systematic about using the months between when managers announce their retirement and when they actually leave to mine and map their knowledge.

These conversations are as important for new leaders promoted within a company as they are for those coming in from the outside. It is too often assumed that someone already working in a business knows why past actions were taken and the circumstances the predecessor was working under. This unstated assumption often makes it impossible for someone to admit what they don't know and ask for help, which is all the more reason to formalize, legitimize, and encourage such conversations.

Support for Internals versus Externals

Throughout this chapter we allude to different approaches for internally promoted general managers versus those hired from the outside. In general, we find that organizations provide better support for external hires. For example, American Express has a robust, consistent assimilation process that is used for all new external executive hires. They are just starting to give a similar level of attention to internally promoted people. It is easier to recognize what external hires don't know and help fill the gaps. Also, external hires often face higher expectations than internal hires and have further to fall when they don't succeed. Usually the company has gone outside because

---

Exhibit 3.3. Preparing a New General Manager to Take Charge

In our consulting practice, we have helped several companies create transition strategies. One particularly effective part of these is coaching new general managers before the transition to think about and plan for the multiple dimensions of their roles that will affect their credibility and effectiveness. Generic questions like those that follow can be used for this purpose.

Introduction to the Organization
- How can I influence the way I am announced in this new role (internally and externally)?
- What is the political climate, and how might it impact this role? Is there controversy around my position or appointment?
- What are the different forums in which I will be introduced and how does the message need to be different for each audience?

Letting Go of the Past Role and Shifting Focus
- How do I make a real transition from my previous role?
- Where do I need to spend my time? How is this different from before?
- What is currently going on in the organization that I need to know more about? How will I find out?
- What pending problems, commitments, or key decisions affect me?
- Are my objectives clear? Are the objectives for the business unit clear?
- What shouldn't I do in this organization?

Building Relationships and a Leadership Brand
- Which key people should I meet?
- Whom can I count on for support?
- How can I reduce the uncertainty among the people in the organization regarding me as their new leader?
- What do others need to know about my style and how I operate?

---

there are no qualified internal candidates and has paid a premium to bring in an external hire.

On the other hand, general managers promoted from functional roles may benefit from a general acknowledgment that this is a stretch or developmental assignment. If the organization has a good talent inventory process, the managers' development needs will be well known and supported. Of course, as we've pointed out, those promoted internally are hampered by the assumption that they know how things operate, have the right relationships, and are well versed in the organizational culture. As a result, adequate attention may be given to filling skill and knowledge needs, but the new boss, colleagues, and HR may underestimate the destabilization and psychological challenge the new general manager is facing. Or they may overlook the unique situation of having to manage former peers and the time and energy required to reestablish credibility and overcome the initial feeling of incompetence.

Many of the approaches and interventions are the same for internal and external hires, although the timing may be different. For example, for an internally promoted general manager, early and immediate action to uncover the concerns of direct reports and begin managing and addressing them is critical. Another high priority is finding a strong replacement in the functional manager role if the new general manager will be supervising his or her former colleagues. For an external hire, a useful step is holding a briefing even before the job starts on the organization's culture and norms, the key players, and how to navigate through informal structures and systems. We particularly like the idea of an "orientation" program, for both external and internal hires, offered sometime between three and six months into the position to allow the still relatively new general managers to get at the questions and issues that have taken on more meaning and urgency now that they have some actual experience under their belts.

Conclusion

It is heartening that although the six challenges discussed above seem to appear consistently across industries, the successful methods of addressing them seem to work equally well in different environments (Downey et al., 2001). Perhaps what we have found most striking in our work with clients and in our research is that, with a few exceptions, most successful transition support practices are fairly simple, low cost, and low tech. They are common-sense interventions that many companies already use in one form or another. Where we see the most impact is when these ideas have been systematized and built into ongoing management practices. This approach not only contributes to individual success but also creates organizational competence.

What is also clear is that this work cannot be delegated to just one person. There are roles for the hiring manager, various levels of HR, specialized talent resources, outside coaches, the promoted manager, and even his or her new team. Linkages to relocation and expatriate support are critical to coordinate transition support for international executives (McCall, 1998). However, it appears that where there is a designated touch point—someone who has the responsibility to manage the process and look out for the success of the new general manager—the pieces come together better. The challenge is to gain the benefits of a centralized, consistent process that can be customized and implemented with a personal touch for each individual general manager.

This requirement of reciprocal interaction is one of the most frequently overlooked aspects of executive transitions in general. The organization needs to be flexible along with the individual if a new general manager is to "fit." The new general manager is a seasoned player—with history, skills, personal characteristics, and experience—encountering an unfamiliar situation. The organization has its own processes, procedures, history, and culture that are fairly stabilized. In order for the transition to be successful, both parties—the new general manager and the organization—need to make adjustments to accommodate the realities of the situation.

Supporting the transition to general manager is a high-return investment for organizations. Much has been written in the past few years about the importance of on-boarding and assimilation, as companies recognize that the amount of time and effort spent during the recruiting and assessment phase has not been matched by the same level of attention post-hire to ensure the new leader's success (Downey et al., 2001). While undeniably helpful, these efforts are often left to the individual's initiative and so, even with this added investment, "sink or swim" continues to be the norm. Since any one manager will make maybe half a dozen significant turns during the course of a career, an organization that depends on individual competence to make these transitions successfully is missing an opportunity, and avoiding a responsibility, to ensure the success of its leaders.

Note

In addition to the many individual general managers and client organizations that we have worked with over the years, we would like to particularly thank the following for providing input for this chapter: Elena Turdo, Head of Executive Orientation at

American Express; Melinda Large, Senior Director of Talent and Development at Wal-Mart; Donna Riechmann, Director of Executive Education and Development at Pfizer; Nancy Buck, Strategic HR Business Partner for Manulife Group Benefits; and Linda Reese, Partner at Executive OnBoarding, LLC. Paul Erickson, of Downey Kates Associates, provided research and editing assistance with this chapter.

References

Brown, S. K. (2003). *Staying ahead of the curve 2003: The AARP working in retirement study.* Washington, DC: AARP Knowledge Management.

Charan, R. (2005). Ending the CEO succession crisis. *Harvard Business Review, 83*(2), 72–81.

Charan, R., Drotter, S., & Noel, J. (2001). *The leadership pipeline: How to build the leadership-powered company.* San Francisco: Jossey-Bass.

Downey, D., March, T., & Berkman, A. (2001). *Assimilating new leaders: The key to executive retention.* New York: AMACOM.

Frank, F. D., Finnegan, R. P., & Taylor, C. R. (2004). The race for talent: Retaining and engaging workers in the 21st century. *Human Resource Planning, 27*(3), 12–25.

Freedman, A. (1998). Pathways and crossroads to institutional leadership. *Consulting Psychology Journal, 50,* 131–151.

Gabarro, J. J. (1987). *The dynamics of taking charge.* Boston: Harvard Business School Press.

Kram, K. E. (1985). *Mentoring at work.* Glenview, IL: Scott, Foresman, and Co.

McCall, M. W., Jr. (1998). *High flyers: Developing the next generation of leaders.* Boston: Harvard Business School Press.

McCall, M. W., Jr., & Lombardo, M. M. (1983). *Off the track: Why and how successful executives get derailed.* Greensboro, NC: Center for Creative Leadership.

McCall, M. W., Jr., Lombardo, M. M., & Morrison, A. M. (1988). *The lessons of experience: How successful executives develop on the job.* Lexington, MA: Lexington Books.

Shipper, F., & Dillard, J. F. (2000). A study of impending derailment and recovery of middle managers across career stages. *Human Resource Management Journal, 39,* 331–345.

Sweeney, P. (1999, February 14). Teaching new hires to feel at home. *New York Times,* p. C4.

Watson Wyatt. (2003). *Demographics and destiny: Winning the war for talent.* Retrieved August 25, 2005, from www.watsonwyatt.com.

When Leadership Development Fails Managers:
Addressing the Right Gaps When Developing Leadership

H. Skipton Leonard
Personnel Decisions International

Recently, a client contacted Personnel Decisions International (PDI) to inquire about its leadership development offerings. In addition to asking about costs and program descriptions, the usual criteria for buying in the past, the vice president for human resources wanted some additional information in order to evaluate PDI's programs:

- What is the underlying process that ensures that people benefit from your leadership development programs?

- How do you identify the people who will benefit most from a leadership development program?

- What is the return on investment (ROI) for your leadership development programs?

In essence, this client was asking the following questions: Do your programs work? Which individuals will benefit the most? Even if you can establish that skills get developed in the program, will that in turn improve organizational performance sufficiently to justify the cost? It seemed apparent that the answers to these questions would be used to convince senior management to invest in a leadership development program in a time when spending every nonproduction, sales, or marketing dollar is subject to the greatest scrutiny.

These questions didn't just come out of the client's mouth; they flowed naturally from a set of underlying assumptions and a particular perspective on leadership development. The first assumption is that a single leadership development process is the basis for all leadership training, from frontline supervisors to executives. That is, the same process can be employed to develop effective leadership competencies and behaviors for all managers, regardless of their place in the organizational hierarchy. A corollary of this assumption is that the success formula—the skills and competencies that lead to effectiveness—is the same at each level of management. Although the expression of these common competencies may be somewhat different at different levels of management (for example, a strategic supervisor might be good at figuring out which production problem is a top priority while a strategic executive might be a master at anticipating how industry trends and emerging regulations create new opportunities), this line of thinking holds that leadership effectiveness is based on the same factors at all levels in the organizational hierarchy.

The second assumption implicit in these questions is that not everyone benefits equally from a given intervention or program. Since leadership development budgets are very tight, it would make sense to invest only in those high potential candidates who would benefit most from the standard approach. While a standard leadership program may very well be the best investment for high potentials, remedial programs may need to be offered for managers who are struggling to master the basics of management—or to help course-correct those managers who are slipping off track, the "derailing" managers identified in early Center for Creative Leadership research (Lombardo & McCauley, 1988; McCall & Lombardo, 1983).

A third assumption is that the client organization may not benefit sufficiently from a formal and costly leadership development program. By asking about ROI, the client is suggesting that any proposed program must clear some predetermined value hurdle to justify an investment in developing leadership skills.

This client's approach to evaluating leadership development programs is common today. Using a single leadership approach simplifies planning and contracting for the company, and program delivery is generally cheaper. When budgets are tight, companies want to spend precious development funds only on the most talented and those most likely to benefit from the process. In this approach, the development of leadership skills is not seen as appropriate or valuable for a broader spectrum of employees.

Another assumption in this perspective is also common even if subtle and less frequently expressed directly. It is popular in HR circles now to disparage traditional training programs and, instead, to advocate developmental assignments, job rotations, mentoring, or nontraditional, structured developmental programs such as action learning and coaching. If consulting and training firms cannot convincingly demonstrate the effectiveness of their leadership development programs in traditional business-value terms, organizations feel justified in saving money by using less costly on-the-job or nontraditional training programs.

An Alternate View

Those evaluating leadership development options, generally HR, training, or organizational development professionals, should be wary of casting the analysis using the questions just posed. I recommend an alternative set of questions to evaluate the value proposition for any proposed leadership development program. These questions follow from two lines of inquiry.

- Does the organization have effective leadership now, and does it have a full "pipeline" of leaders for the future? If not, where are the current and future gaps in leadership capabilities? What skills are required to fill these gaps?

- How do people best learn complex skills like leadership? What is the evidence that a particular development technique or intervention will have the desired impact? What are the best ways to evaluate the success of leadership development programs?

I would argue that the underlying assumptions for these questions are not only more persuasive in terms of building a business case but also more consistent with what we know about leadership and adult development. These assumptions include that (1) leadership is vital to the success of the organization, (2) different gaps and learning needs require different solutions, and (3) a successful solution is based on a valid model of adult development.

Posing these questions and addressing the underlying assumptions in this way shift the discussion away from a purely tactical "prove that your model works" to one that is more strategic and focused on the organization's broader current and future leadership needs. Framing the analysis and debate in these latter terms compared to the initial ones prevents HR, training, or organizational development advocates for leadership development from taking a defensive posture. Since ROI for any long-term developmental program is difficult to establish, the conversations are frequently reduced to considerations of efficiency, simplicity, and cost. This is not a favorable battleground for discussing effective leadership development programming.

Making the Case for a Strategic Approach to Leadership Development

The major failing of the first set of questions and assumptions posed by the client, if not followed up with the additional questions, is that there is no apparent linkage between leadership development and the mission, vision, or business strategy of the organization. The questions imply a unitary, one-size-fits-all approach to leadership regardless of context—what skills, what prognosis (development, remedial), or what organizational level. They also beg the following questions: Do we really need to invest in a formal leadership development program at all? Can't the organization just rely on on-the-job training experiences such as developmental and stretch assignments, job rotations, or lightly structured programs such as mentoring, coaching, and action learning projects to meet our current and future leadership needs? Further, if the organization does decide to provide leadership development programming, can it minimize costs by targeting a smaller group of individuals, high potentials, who are perceived to be our future senior leaders?

My purpose is not to dismiss or discredit any of these legitimate questions. However, these are primarily tactical questions focused on efficiency, simplicity, and cost. In addition to these tactical concerns, leadership development programs should be evaluated in relation to their effectiveness in developing leadership talent at all levels of the organization. The performance of the organization does not rest solely on the performance of a small subset of high potential managers. As DeLong and Vijayaraghavan (2003) have noted, organizational success depends as much on having a strong bench of competent B managers as having a small group of star A players. The performance of the organization overall requires solid functioning at the supervisory, functional, middle management, and executive levels. Without addressing the gaps in leadership skills for managers and leaders at all levels of the organization, the enterprise is unlikely to achieve its strategic vision, goals, and mission (Boudreau & Ramstad, 2003).

One Model Does Not Fit All

Freedman, in chapter 2 and elsewhere (Freedman, 1998), makes a compelling case for the proposition that different challenges and thus different skills are required to successfully navigate a career stretching from individual contributor to institutional leader. Charan, Drotter, and Noel (2001) have based their recommendations for building a "leadership pipeline" on similar arguments. At each critical promotional crossroad in a leader's career (see figure 2.1), leaders must go through a personal, transformational change by letting go (with respect and appreciation) of some skills that were crucial to their success in lower levels of the organization while maintaining other skills that continue to be relevant and adding new skills to address the unfamiliar challenges they encounter in higher levels of the organization.

It follows that leadership programs should help managers not only learn new skills but also let go of some skills or certain responsibilities that will be counterproductive in their quest for effectiveness and excellence. That is, both learning and unlearning are distinct pedagogical goals. Freedman describes the process of unlearning in terms of the psychological process of withdrawal from an addiction in which managers must grieve and mourn the loss of skills and abilities that got them noticed and promoted in the organization earlier in their careers.

A recent study by Kaiser and Craig (2004; see also the introduction) provides convincing empirical evidence to support Freedman's thesis that the profile of skills and competencies that lead to success changes with management level. Their analysis of a large multirater database including over 2,000 managers from dozens of companies representing fifteen industries clearly indicates that the success formula differs significantly depending upon the position of the leader in the organizational hierarchy. The following profiles describe the unique blend of characteristics associated with effectiveness Kaiser and Craig found at three distinct organizational levels.

Bottom Level

Successful supervisors were good at setting boundaries between work and their personal lives. They were described as moderately decisive and somewhat micromanaging and, although likable and nonabrasive, interpersonally distant from their subordinates. They lacked follow-through, indicating that they had not yet developed strong project management skills.

Middle Level

Successful middle managers were more decisive and interpersonally warm, less distant from their subordinates than supervisors. Boundaries between work and personal life became more blurred for middle managers. They were seen as slightly more empowering and better at follow-through than supervisors, but these factors weren't strong positive predictors of their overall effectiveness. These findings suggest that middle managers are still developing their ability to delegate and lead through influence rather than authority. They also continue to struggle with the issues of project management and execution.

Top Level

Successful executives were far less decisive than middle managers and supervisors, suggesting that they had learned to be reflective and to research situations thoroughly before acting or making decisions. They also used a much more participatory style and involved others in decision making and discussing complex issues. Work took on a priority in the life of the successful executive, and the boundaries between work and personal life dissolved. At the executive level, interpersonal warmth and its destructive cousin, abrasiveness, were not related to effectiveness. Executives were much better in the areas of empowerment and follow-through than either middle managers or supervisors. These results suggest that executives have learned how to get things done through people by mastering the art of motivating and inspiring others. They have also learned how to translate high-level ideas of mission, vision, and strategy into executable plans.

Only one skill of the seven Kaiser and Craig (2004) investigated was consistently associated with managerial effectiveness at the bottom, middle, and top. That was an active learning orientation. However, this skill was more related to success at the supervisor and executive level than at the middle manager level. One explanation for this finding is that the middle management role is one of "interpolation of structure" (Katz & Kahn, 1966)— translating vision, mission, and strategy into operating goals, implementation plans, and project management. These activities may require less of a learning orientation than the supervisor role with its emphasis on pragmatic innovation or the executive role, where more conceptual and synthetic thinking is required. Kaiser and Craig note that these findings are generally consistent with a wealth of descriptive models that characterize the changing nature of managerial work across levels (Hunt, 1991; Jaques, 1976; Katz & Kahn, 1966; Zaccaro, 2001).

Recall that the client described at the beginning of this chapter asked, "How do you identify the people who will benefit most from a leadership development program?" As I have just argued, organizations need to develop the leadership skills for all supervisors, middle managers, and executives as well as managers at different levels of proficiency, not just an elite group of high potentials. As Freedman (1998) has persuasively argued and Kaiser and Craig (2004) have demonstrated, the programmatic strategies need to be tailored to the particular needs and career stage of the supervisor, manager, and executive. At a given point in time, supervisors, managers, or executives may be working to master the set of unique skills required for that role and organizational level (that is, going through the process of adding, maintaining, or letting go of certain behaviors), or they may have mastered these behaviors and skills and may be ready for promotion to the next level. Leaders who are underperforming and who need to master skills at their current levels may benefit most from targeted interventions such as skills training. This is a much more focused and efficient approach to development for these leaders. This is especially true for individuals who are having difficulty mastering specific competencies or who are finding it difficult to let go of some cherished skills. Leaders ready for promotion may benefit most from more formal, comprehensive, and extended leadership development programs along with the kind of transition preparation described in chapter 3.

Organizations should also consider providing basic leadership and management training for all employees entering the ranks of supervisors and managers. Too many organizations now reserve specialized leadership and management training for the elite few who are designated as high potentials. As a result, many supervisors and managers are now expected to learn necessary leadership and management skills on the job while receiving little formal exposure to the basic principles and little opportunity to develop and practice new skills.

How Transformational Leadership Dazzled Us

Transformational leadership, the approach inspired by James MacGregor Burns's (1978) Pulitzer prize–winning book, *Leadership*, has had a tight grip on both leadership theory and practice for the past quarter century. There is good reason for this stranglehold; the evidence for the effectiveness of transformational leadership is striking and quite remarkable. Before Burns, "transactional" models of leadership held sway in the field of leadership development. Transactional models hold that successful leaders focus on making sure employees receive equitable rewards and benefits in exchange for meeting the expectations of the manager and organization. Burns distinguished transformational leadership from transactional leadership, noting that the latter may be sufficient for understanding typical, day-to-day exchanges between managers and employees but is wholly inadequate for understanding extraordinary performance. Transformational leadership was offered to explain how leaders inspire performance beyond expectations. Bass (1998) has elaborated Burns's notion of transformational leadership and identified several key behavioral dimensions that define it. This behavior-based definition and distinction between the two approaches to leadership are presented in exhibit 4.1.

Exhibit 4.1. The Dimensions of Transformational and Transactional Leadership

Transformational Leadership
- Idealized influence (charisma): The leader is perceived as trustworthy and capable of achieving an important vision.
- Inspirational motivation: The leader has the ability to communicate an inspiring vision.
- Intellectual stimulation: The leader challenges past ideas and supports independent thinking and creativity.
- Individualized consideration: The leader treats followers fairly but recognizes individuality and treats accordingly.

Transactional Leadership
- Contingent reward: The leader positively rewards desired behavior, punishing or sanctioning undesirable behavior.
- Management by exception: The leader intervenes only when something goes wrong.

Note. These dimensions and their definitions are based on the work of Bernard Bass (1998).

The business press has seen its share of popular books that extol the kind of transformational leadership described by Burns (1978), including Kouzes and Posner's (1987) *The Leadership Challenge* and Tichy and Devanna's (1986) *The Transformational Leader*. This popular endorsement is supported by a truly impressive body of research. This work empirically establishes the advantages of transformational over transactional leadership. In the field of behavior science where correlations of .35 are seen as solid and .50 very strong, studies (called meta-analyses) that quantify the trend across dozens of independent studies of transformational leadership find average correlations between transformational factors and leadership effectiveness in the .55 to .75 range. For example, Lowe, Kroeck, and Sivasubramaniam (1996) reported the meta-analytic estimates of the relationships between dimensions of transformational and transactional leadership and effectiveness in private and public sector organizations, as reported in exhibit 4.2.

Exhibit 4.2. Correlations between Leadership and Effectiveness in Public and Private Organizations

Leadership Style	Sector	
	Public	Private
Transformational		
Charismatic	.74	.69
Intellectual stimulation	.65	.56
Individual consideration	.63	.62
Transactional		
Contingent reward	.41	.41
Management by exception	.10	-.02

Note. These results are based on a meta-analysis published by Lowe, Kroeck, and Sivasubramaniam (1996).

A previous meta-analysis of twenty studies of transformational and transactional leadership by Gasper (1992) reported correlations of the same magnitude. Gasper estimated that the correlation between an overall transformational factor (the average of all transformation dimensions) correlated .76, .71, and .88 for three measures of leadership outcomes: perceived leadership effectiveness, subordinates' satisfaction with leadership, and the degree of extra effort from subordinates. The respective estimated mean-corrected correlations for transactional leadership were .27, .22, and .32 respectively.

The results from these analyses are remarkable, and the demonstrated virtues of transformational leadership gained this approach dominance in the theory of leadership and the practice of leadership development. While other leadership models such as situational leadership (Hersey & Blanchard, 1969) continued to be a mainstay for many training departments in the 1980s, by the 1990s most newly developed leadership development programs were based on the transformational leadership model.

In recent years, prominent thought leaders such as John Kotter (1990, 1996) have written compellingly about the differences between management and leadership. The role of a manager is seen as planning and budgeting, organizing, directing, and controlling. Leaders, on the other hand, are expected to establish purpose and direction, align people and efforts, and inspire and empower the organization. Managers are seen as merely administrators coping with complexity and trying to do things right (Bennis, 1989), while leaders are catalysts for change and heroically go against the grain to do the right thing. From this perspective, management, being concerned with control, is equivalent to Burns's (1978) and Bass's (1998) notion of transactional leadership whereas leadership, with its emphasis on change, is tantamount to transformational leadership.

Although there is an attempt to provide balance and note the value of transactional leadership, the message is clear—organizations need to place a priority on developing transformational leaders. Leadership, it seems, is in, while management is, de facto, out. Accordingly, young supervisors and managers who want to get ahead should focus on developing transformational skills.

By the year 2000, the acceptance of the transformational model as the one best model for leadership was very high. I have observed, in recent years, that the number of training programs in organizations focusing on basic management skills has declined dramatically while leadership development programs stressing transformational leadership skills have proliferated. As a result, training programs from the supervisory to executive levels have been primarily teaching how to be transformational leaders and giving the transactional leadership and basic management skills taught in traditional training courses of yesteryear little attention.

You Need to Learn to Crawl Before You're Ready to Run

From the earlier discussion of the differences in challenges and necessary skills at various levels of the organization (Freedman, 1998; Kaiser & Craig, 2004), one should be skeptical of any approach that promotes one best way to lead. It should be noted that proponents of transformational leadership never promoted this approach to the exclusion of transactional leadership. Bass (1998), for instance, recommends a Full Range of Leadership Model. Bass corrected the balance in emphasis between transactional and transformational leadership this way:

> Transactional leadership, particularly contingent reward, provides a
> broad basis for effective leadership, but a greater amount of effort,

effectiveness, and satisfaction is possible from transactional leadership if augmented by transformational leadership . . . transformational leadership also augments transactional in predicting levels of innovation, risk-taking and creativity. (Bass, 1998, p. 10)

While Bass's Full Range of Leadership Model suggests a situational leadership approach, it does not indicate which transactional or transformational leadership behaviors are ideal for which leadership situations or at which particular level of the organization.

In revisiting the results reported by Kaiser and Craig (2004), it is instructive to note that the leadership behaviors displayed by effective executives fall on the transformational leadership end of the Full Range of Leadership Model suggested by Bass (1998), while the behaviors exhibited by supervisors are clearly more transactional in nature. This suggests that transformational leadership is more appropriate and effective at senior levels, while transactional leadership plays a primary role lower in the organization. Supervisors, working on the front lines and struggling to get former peers to accept their new power and authority, set clear boundaries with respect to emotional involvement with direct reports, work, and their personal lives. At the same time, they are careful to maintain positive work relationships with their direct reports, are task oriented and closely control the work process, and focus on short-term success.

Middle managers, charged with executing the strategic plan to make the executive leadership vision a reality, demonstrate a blend of mostly transactional and some modest degree of transformational behaviors. They retain the bias toward action and quick decision making while maintaining positive relationships with employees and colleagues and improving their ability to execute longer-term tactical plans. Yet vision and empowerment—central aspects of transformational leadership—are not key ingredients in the success formula for middle managers.

Effective executives recognize that they must be most concerned about creating a vision and developing strategy. Success involves applying seasoned judgment and deliberation on a few strategic decisions. Successful executives, therefore, are more reflective and slower to make decisions and take actions; they also realize that in order to get work done through people, they must have a strong team and a larger workforce that feels empowered. Effective executives know that it is more important to be respected by employees for integrity, fairness, and competence than for being likable and popular. This description of what Kaiser and Craig (2004) found to characterize effective supervisors, middle managers, and executives is consistent with

Kotter's (1996) conclusions that supervisors and managers are fundamentally concerned with control and doing things right while executives are more focused on change and doing the right things.

A strong argument can be made that the transformational leadership model, as effective as it is in many situations, has been oversold and that the fields of leadership and leadership development need to go further in establishing how the Full Range of Leadership Model that Bass (1998) recommends plays out at different levels of management. It is essentially a "one best way" model, whereas several lines of thinking and empirical study converge in suggesting the need for an approach to leadership and its development that is tailored to the organizational level in which it is taking place.

A summary of the literature and research on transformational and transactional leadership, as well as the changing organizational challenges and skill requirements at different organizational levels (Charan et al., 2001; Freedman, 1998) and the unique characteristics of successful supervisors, middle managers, and executives (Kaiser & Craig, 2004), indicates that distinctly different kinds of leadership skills, learning techniques, and approaches to leadership development are required for managers at different levels of the organization and at different stages in their careers. While it is beyond the scope of this chapter to describe in any detail what the development offerings should look like at each level in a manager's career, chapters 2, 3, and 5 provide an outline and description of the competencies that are necessary for success across the hierarchy.

ROI Is the Wrong Question

Do companies ask the accounting function for the ROI for the budgeting or auditing processes? Of course not! They don't have to because there is overwhelming consensus that a company needs to have these processes to effectively manage the business and satisfy regulatory requirements. Furthermore, if companies were required to provide the ROI for these processes, they probably couldn't because of the lack of a direct causal relationship between these processes and procedures and profitability.

Similarly, asking for the ROI on a leadership development program is the wrong question. I think the more appropriate question is, What would be the consequences of not having a formal process for developing leaders for the future? I am quite confident that senior management, posed this question, would quickly come to the conclusion that having no process for developing leadership is not an option. As Weik (chapter 1) reports, many CEOs understand this and take leadership development to be self-evidently valuable.

Furthermore, using ROI as the primary way to evaluate a leadership program focuses on tactical issues such as efficiency and cost rather than strategic considerations of how the organization can best achieve its strategic vision, goals, and mission (Boudreau & Ramstad, 2003). Linking leadership development to strategic imperatives establishes the legitimacy of the investment and advances discussions to the next logical level of decision making. Once the necessity of formal leadership development programming is established, the next critical question is, How do people learn complex skills like leadership best?

In answering this question, Hicks and Peterson's (1999) discussion of the necessary and sufficient conditions for effective human development and learning is useful. These authors identified a "development pipeline" composed of insight, motivation, capability development, real-world practice, and accountability, which are the active ingredients that determine the amount of development that actually results from an organization's developmental programming. Each element addresses a different requirement and is a potential "pinch point" for development. Instead of demanding the ROI for leadership development, clients should carefully consider how effective the proposed program is in addressing each of the required elements for effective development identified by Hicks and Peterson. Moreover, the question of value cannot be determined without considering the entire developmental pipeline. A great classroom leadership development experience is of little value, for instance, if participants have little opportunity to practice new leadership skills in a real-world environment.

A Client Tells Us How to Improve

We recently completed two leadership development classes for a nonprofit research organization and demonstrated significant positive impact for the organization as a whole (Leonard & Goff, 2003). The organizational sponsor for the program was quite sophisticated in the field of leadership and had set objectives for the program that were clearly designed to develop transformational leadership skills. The emphasis in the program was upon visionary and strategic thinking, creativity, collaboration, and inspirational leadership. Much less emphasis was given to the more mundane transactional leadership "blocking and tackling" skills such as planning, delegating, and monitoring performance. Participants went through the program as cohorts and included scientific team leaders, middle managers, and the senior leaders of the organization. The participants were considered the present and future leadership for the organization. Few had received any exposure to either management training or leadership development, so including participants from several levels in the organization seemed reasonable.

Before we started the third class, the client provided some feedback and guidance for modification of the program to make it more effective. In debriefing the first two programs, the client noted that while senior leader and middle manager participants from the first programs were enthusiastic about the program, the team leader participants felt that the program was not practical enough. They had some difficulty applying the skills and concepts that we presented to the challenges they faced in their roles. Since the new class had a higher percentage of team leaders and middle managers than the first two classes, the program was redesigned to include more focus on transactional leadership skills.

This experience was in keeping with the theoretical framework developed in this chapter. Leadership development is not a unitary process, and different approaches to leadership development are required at each point along the promotional pathway for each leader.

Meeting the Needs of Both Participant and Organization

Leadership development programs fail to deliver on organizational and participant expectations when they (1) are based on one best way—either one best prescriptive model of leadership or one best way to impart learning and skills development, (2) are not based on valid and effective models for adult learning and development, and (3) take a tactical approach by emphasizing efficiency, simplicity, cost, and ROI rather than a more strategic approach that considers the current and future gaps in leadership capabilities and the impact of these deficits upon achievement of strategic goals. By reframing the concerns about leadership development in more strategic terms, HR and organizational development leaders can demonstrate the real value of their programs and avoid being trapped in a defensive position of having to prove that their recommendations are worth the investment.

Note

PDI has deep expertise and over thirty-five years of experience in both the assessment and development of executive and managerial leadership talent in local, national, and global corporations and organizations.

References

Bass, B. M. (1998). *Transformational leadership: Industrial, military, and educational impact.* Mahwah, NJ: Lawrence Erlbaum Associates.

Bennis, W. B. (1989). *Why leaders can't lead.* San Francisco: Jossey-Bass.

Boudreau, J. W., & Ramstad, P. M. (2003). Strategic I/O psychology and the role of utility analysis models. In W. Borman, D. Ilgen, & R. Klimoski (Eds.), *Handbook of psychology: Vol. 12. Industrial-organizational psychology.* Hoboken, NJ: Wiley.

Burns, J. M. (1978). *Leadership.* New York: Harper.

Charan, R., Drotter, S., & Noel, J. (2001). *The leadership pipeline: How to build the leadership-powered company.* San Francisco: Jossey-Bass.

DeLong, T. J., & Vijayaraghavan, V. (2003, June). Let's hear it for B players. *Harvard Business Review,* 96–102.

Freedman, A. M. (1998). Pathways and crossroads to institutional leadership. *Consulting Psychology Journal, 50*(3), 131–151.

Gasper, J. M. (1992). Transformational leadership: An integrative review of the literature. (Doctoral dissertation, Western Michigan State University, 1992). *Dissertation Abstracts International, 53,* 2619.

Hersey, P., & Blanchard, K. (1969). Life cycle theory of leadership. *Training and Development Journal, 2,* 6–34.

Hicks, M. D., & Peterson, D. E. (1999). The development pipeline: How people really learn. *Knowledge Management Review, 9,* 30–33.

Hunt, J. G. (1991). *Leadership: A new synthesis.* Newbury Park, CA: Sage Publications.

Jaques, E. (1976). *A general theory of bureaucracy.* London: Heinemann.

Kaiser, R. B., & Craig, S. B. (2004, April). What gets you there won't keep you there: Managerial behaviors related to effectiveness at the bottom, middle, and top. In R. B. Kaiser & S. B. Craig (Cochairs), *Filling the pipe I: Studying management development across the hierarchy.* Symposium presented at the Nineteenth Annual Conference of the Society for Industrial and Organizational Psychology, Chicago.

Katz, D., & Kahn, R. L. (1966). *The social psychology of organizations* (1st ed.). New York: Wiley.

Kotter, J. P. (1990). *A force for change: How leadership differs from management.* New York: Free Press.

Kotter, J. P. (1996). *Leading change.* Boston: Harvard Business School Press.

Kouzes, J. M., & Posner, B. Z. (1987). *The leadership challenge: How to get extraordinary things done in organizations.* San Francisco: Jossey-Bass.

Leonard, H. S., & Goff, M. (2003). Leadership development as an intervention for organizational transformation. *Consulting Psychology Journal, 55,* 58–67.

Lombardo, M. M., & McCauley, C. (1988). *The dynamics of management derailment.* Greensboro, NC: Center for Creative Leadership.

Lowe, K., Kroeck, K. G., & Sivasubramaniam, N. (1996). Effectiveness correlates of transformational and transactional leadership: A meta-analytic review. *Leadership Quarterly, 7,* 385–425.

McCall, M. W., & Lombardo, M. M. (1983). *Off the track: Why and how successful executives get derailed.* Greensboro, NC: Center for Creative Leadership.

Tichy, N., & Devanna, M. (1986). *The transformational leader: Molding tomorrow's corporate winners.* New York: Wiley.

Zaccaro, S. J. (2001). *The nature of executive leadership: A conceptual and empirical analysis of success.* Washington, DC: American Psychological Association.

Creating Synergy and Difference in Development: One Organization's Competencies for Three Organizational Levels

Jennifer Martineau, Greg Laskow, and Lisa Moye
Center for Creative Leadership

Dick Phillips
Central Intelligence Agency

The previous chapters in this volume clearly make a case for taking organizational level into account in the development of leaders. Chapter 2 illustrates how level transitions pose a significant adaptive challenge to individual managers. It goes on to demonstrate this with the unique case of becoming a CEO. Chapter 3 applies this logic to the more common transition of becoming a general manager. And chapter 4 is persuasive in advocating a more strategic view of the role of leadership development, a view that emphasizes the distinction between lower-level management skills and senior-level leadership skills. The purpose of this chapter is to present a case example of what it means to adopt such a perspective and implement it. Specifically, we describe the steps the Central Intelligence Agency (CIA or Agency) took in transforming its approach to leadership by identifying a set of competencies that custom-fit both the organization and three unique levels of management. It is an approach that recognizes the common challenges facing the organization as a whole while also respecting the unique demands of supervisor, middle manager, and executive positions.

To be sure, the CIA is in many ways a unique organization. At the same time, many of the challenges it faces are familiar to any large organization trying to navigate a bureaucracy intended to create order through a turbulent global environment that demands flexibility and agility. And so it is our hope that this example will provide some fresh ideas and practical suggestions for those responsible for filling a deep and talented pool of future leaders in other organizations.

A Unified Effort

On the surface, it would appear that many organizations already take hierarchical-level differences into account. After all, the selection process—

where candidates come from, who is involved in the decision process, what kinds of assessment data are sought—is quite different at the top of the house than it is in lower ranks (Sessa, Kaiser, Taylor, & Campbell, 1998). Some organizations even have distinct leadership development processes in operation at different levels of management. Your organization may have a different approach for middle managers compared to senior executives, for example. So there is some degree of differentiation. But what is often missing is integration. Development initiatives at different organizational levels are usually created in isolation, and for many reasons:

- There may be no overall development strategy encompassing the whole organization.

- Different individuals or teams are responsible for the design, development, and delivery of the development processes at each level.

- Programs are designed, developed, and delivered during different time periods.

- The value in creating alignment across the processes used for different levels isn't obvious.

The list goes on and on. But in the end, failure to integrate development efforts leads to the creation of strategies that, at the very least, aren't coordinated and, at the extreme, are inconsistent and create unnecessary confusion. Participants in these programs may see a connection between their training and development and the demands of their current roles. Or, as chapter 4 points out, they may not—the intervention may not have been designed around the unique features of their current roles. Either way, confusion and discord arise when moving upward to a job of greater responsibility. As chapter 2 illustrates, upward transitions are already fraught with difficulty because of the significant change and discontinuity in what is required for success. This difficulty is compounded by a lack of continuity in leadership education, assessment, and development.

Another risk organizations face in the absence of an integrated curriculum is failing to garner the support of executive decision makers and other key stakeholders who influence funding decisions for training and development efforts. Like Leonard (chapter 4), we also take a strategic view of the company-wide value of a fully integrated leadership development system. With increasing frequency, senior leaders are demanding evidence that development initiatives are worth the cost. It is more difficult to establish value when the various pieces are disparate and lack a common framework.

And linking a haphazard and disconnected system to strategy is virtually impossible. An integrated system, however, provides more efficiency, clearer evaluation metrics, and more obvious links to supporting business needs.

In the end, organizational effectiveness is at stake. Without integration, development systems can inadvertently hamper performance and be harmful when they create confusion about what is needed and expected in a given role. So the question arises: how can leadership development systems that already exist or are coming online be integrated?

We suggest that competency models can be tools for integrating leadership development processes across an organization. We have found that this can work when the model includes a common core reflecting leadership needs facing the whole company and also emphasizes the unique demands facing distinctly different groups of managers. You might think of it as customized integration.

How the CIA Did It

As a governmental agency responsible to the executive branch of the U.S. government and as an agency that is responsive to the ever-changing geopolitical events of the world, the CIA has the perennial challenge of developing leaders. In 2002, the president of the CIA's "corporate" university decided that the leadership development curriculum for supervisors, middle managers, and directors should be revised. There were several reasons for the revision, and achieving alignment across the curriculum was a particularly influential goal. Following the cataclysmic events of September 11, 2001, the Agency came under intense internal and external scrutiny. The implications for failures in leadership were suddenly intensified enormously. This made leader development a strategic priority. The alignment and integration process enabled the Agency's Leadership Academy to retain many existing development offerings while inserting updated components that addressed newer organizational challenges. There are parallel forces, although perhaps less dramatic, in the private sector as well that can create organizational readiness for integrated leadership development. Organizational takeovers and mergers, increased and intense external competition, and rapid organizational growth are among the many forces our client organizations experience.

The CIA's senior executives truly understood the need for a curriculum that built upon itself, highlighting the significant differences and areas of overlap across levels of management. Like a third of the CEOs described in the RHR survey discussed in chapter 1, these leaders recognized the inherent value of the role leadership development played in the larger organizational strategy. In particular, they wanted to create supporting guidance for a career ladder for employees. In addition, they also understood how having managers at one level understand the development needs of their employees at the level below would, for instance, make coaching and mentoring easier. They also saw the importance of their corps of managers understanding the unique role of leadership in more senior jobs, to facilitate upward transitions, as described in chapters 2 and 3. Hence, the Leadership Academy proceeded with a needs assessment process that took stock of the organization's strategic position and allowed a gap analysis of where their leadership capacity was compared to where it needed to be. The audit included separate considerations of leadership needs at the supervisory, middle, and senior leader levels. The process resulted in the identification of a common set of organizational challenges that were then translated into leadership needs and competencies for these three different populations of managers. The resulting set of competencies across each of the three levels has consistency of purpose—namely, the key strategic business needs that provided a rationale for leadership development—and appropriate overlap and distinction across levels.

The needs assessment was designed by colleagues at CCL: Kathleen Ponder, Ellie Hall, Davida Sharpe, and Jennifer Martineau. It is a generic process that can be adapted, if not in whole at least in part, to the creation or modification of most leadership development systems. The Leadership Development Impact Assessment (LDIA) is a facilitated two-day process with seven distinct steps that lead to a conceptual design for the delivery and evaluation of programs and processes. It results in a report documenting the output from the process. The output of each step is described below. Exhibit 5.1 describes the seven steps and the purpose and outcome of those steps.

Analyzing the Business Need

The LDIA process begins at the organizational challenge level, with the identification of the most critical organizational-level issues that prompted the CIA to turn to CCL and leadership development as a solution. In our work with the CIA, these challenges were identified by a diverse group of CIA employees and contractors, many of whom were or once had been members of the Leadership Academy staff; some were employed by one of the three main departments: operations, intelligence, and analysis. Before joining the Leadership Academy, most staff members had been employed by one or more of the three departments.

Exhibit 5.1. CCL's Leadership Development Impact Assessment (LDIA) Process

Step 1: Analyzing the Business Need

With the focus group, CCL faculty members review the internal summary of business needs. The CCL facilitator probes to ensure business needs affecting all potential participant groups have been identified and then poses the following question: What are the top three business needs that must be met? A forced-choice exercise produces a business needs "bull's-eye," a keen focus on the most critical needs. If time or money become limited, it is important to know which business needs and associated leadership development processes can and cannot be sacrificed.

Step 2: Identifying Leadership Needs and Structural or Systems Needs

The group probes to delineate specific prevalent leader behaviors and attitudes associated with leadership needs. The group answers this question: How are your leaders' behaviors preventing you from meeting this business need? The next exercise uncovers structural or systems needs that also must be addressed in order to meet the business needs and leverage CCL's leadership development work: What other organizational practices must be addressed to meet your business need?

Step 3: Setting Critical Leadership Priorities

The focus group determines the relative importance of each of the leadership needs through a prioritization exercise. Because time and money are always limited, cuts may be needed in the leadership development program length and/or content. This exercise illuminates which leadership needs can and can't be sacrificed.

Step 4: Identifying Research-Based Leader Competencies

CCL has compiled a research-based database capturing what effective corporate leaders actually think, feel, and do. This exercise matches the competencies from CCL's research-based Model of Leader Competencies to each of the leadership needs. The chosen competencies and associated outcomes are compiled into a final list, providing targeted learning for all programs and processes.

(continued)

**Exhibit 5.1. CCL's Leadership Development Impact
Assessment (LDIA) Process (cont.)**

Step 5: Determining Levels of Mastery

Using CCL's levels-of-mastery model, the focus group assigns to each leadership competency a mastery level target. They answer the following questions: What level of mastery do we want? Is it okay for participants to have awareness and basic knowledge about the leadership competency, or do we want them to be able to skillfully perform this competency back in the workplace? A mastery level is assigned to each leadership competency.

Step 6: Conceptualizing the Delivery Framework

This exercise conceptualizes, in a broad-brush way, how delivery of the initiative will look over time. During the impact assessment phase, the focus group will conceptualize the number of events, their length, and the kinds of delivery events acceptable to their culture, based on the leadership competency targets chosen and the level of mastery desired for each. This step concludes with a concept "drawing"—a framework—of the initiative.

Step 7: Conceptualizing the Evaluation Process

This last step determines the kinds of evidence major client stakeholders will accept as proof of program impact and the types of data needing to be gathered. The focus group answers questions such as these: Do our stakeholders want normative group assessment profiles showing how our leaders compare to leaders in similar industries? Do they want survey results showing how fellow workers see the participants behaving differently as leaders six months after the program?

Organizational challenges are identified through a series of questions that require participants to describe the current pressures on the organization, either as a whole or as separate entities. When the list of resulting organizational challenges is large (more than five), participants are guided through a process of prioritization that results in a smaller number of challenges. This is important because the group must be clear what forces it is trying to address through leadership development, and those forces should be the most pressing. If time or money available for the leadership development initiative is limited, it is important to know which organizational challenges can and cannot be sacrificed.

At the conclusion of this step, the result was a narrowed list of organizational challenges the CIA faced at that time and/or was expected to face in the near future (see "Content of the Models" on page 99).

Identifying Leadership Needs and Structural or Systems Needs

The second step connected the organizational-level challenges to leadership needs and challenges—asking what leadership shortfalls are preventing leaders from addressing the organizational challenges. It is at this step that each target group of leaders is considered separately, in separate LDIA sessions. This is how the customization for each level occurred. We have found that it is too difficult to try to identify development needs and create a high-level program design for multiple groups simultaneously. For the purpose of illustration, we describe the remaining steps by focusing on one group: middle managers (the competency outcomes for all three groups are found in exhibit 5.2, presented and described on pages 102–103). For the other levels (supervisors and executives), the process was identical for steps 2–7.

When identifying leadership needs for the middle management population, the group was asked, "How are your leaders' behaviors preventing you from meeting this organizational challenge?" Twenty-four leadership needs were named and included behaviors such as creating a safe learning environment, pushing decision making to the lowest possible levels, and working within the bureaucracy to accomplish innovation. These leadership needs are captured in the words of the client group—they do not come from any predetermined lists.

In the process of naming leadership behaviors or challenges, participants inevitably want to name organizational systems or structures that must be addressed in order to effectively work on the organizational challenges. For example, we often hear about information technology challenges, performance evaluation systems, and communication processes. It is important to get these factors named and listed so that leadership development sponsors are aware of the potential barriers to success and can work with the appropriate group(s) to address them. In fact, we have worked with clients who have incorporated those systems and structural challenges into the leadership development effort itself in the form of an action learning project, asking participants to study the issues and make recommendations for improvements as part of their developmental experience.

Setting Critical Leadership Priorities

The third step taken with our group from the CIA was to prioritize the leadership challenges and reduce them to a manageable number before moving to the fourth step: identifying leadership competencies. Because time and money are rarely unlimited, organizations usually need to determine the most critical leadership needs on which to focus their work. This is done through a rank-ordering process in which each participant ranks the leadership needs they perceive to be the five most important to address. This exercise illuminates which leadership needs can and can't be sacrificed. A final set of leadership needs identified for the manager group included the following:

- Model effective leadership behaviors.

- Speak and listen effectively and respectfully.

- Think systemically (and understand their role in the system).

- See their role as developing and teaching others.

- Build an effective management team.

- Have standards (and articulate and live by them), trust, and integrity.

Identifying Research-Based Leader Competencies

In this fourth step, the CIA team was guided through a card-sort process to identify the specific competencies critical to preparing leaders to address the organizational challenges. The competencies captured in the deck of cards originate from several sources and comprise CCL's Model of Leader Competencies. The bulk of the competencies come from CCL's 360 by Design Web-based, customizable 360-degree assessment instrument, which includes the scales (that is, competencies) from multiple CCL 360-degree assessment instruments and models. Each of these assessments rests on a foundation of research that produced the scales included on it. In addition, it includes other competencies that come from CCL research but are not part of a unique assessment instrument.

It is worth noting that the competencies included in CCL's Model of Leader Competencies have significant overlap with those found in other competency taxonomies such as those created by Personnel Decisions International, Lominger Ltd., the Hay Group, and others. In fact, when competency taxonomies are as thorough as these are, it is believed that they cover the vast majority of all possible leadership competencies. For instance, Mike Lombardo and Bob Eichinger (2002) have studied this question and concluded that the competencies needed to perform effectively as a manager are about 85 percent the same across different job situations. They emphasize that what may change is the relative importance of competencies, which we take up in the next section on levels of mastery. For the most part, the kinds of knowledge, skills, and abilities needed for success as a manager are known. Readers are encouraged not to feel compelled to develop their own competencies from scratch; there are enough adequate competency libraries available that it would be inefficient to create a new one from scratch.

To select the competencies to include in the model, the CIA group was divided into subgroups of three or four members each. Each subgroup was tasked with identifying the competencies most relevant to the prioritized set of leadership needs. Once each group completed that task, their recommendations were captured in a matrix that enabled the group to see the agreement and disagreement in their selections. In the discussion that followed, the CIA group settled on thirty-three competencies that they believed were important for success at the middle management level and should be addressed in some way during the leadership development initiative for this level (see exhibit 5.2, pages 102–103).

Determining Levels of Mastery

At this point, savvy readers may be questioning our judgment. "Thirty-three competencies: are they crazy?" Rest assured that we entered the next phase with a clear understanding that thirty-three competencies are too many to address sufficiently during a leadership development initiative. That is where levels of mastery come in.

During this step, the competencies were differentiated in terms of the level of mastery required—that is, the level of proficiency needed to perform each competency. We used a four-tiered system for this. First is the critical awareness and knowledge level, which involves being intellectually familiar with the competency and having a deep awareness of one's own performance in a particular area (competency), its impact on others, and the relationship between one's own competency and that needed to effectively do the work. Next is guided application, the ability to practice and use the new competency in a safe setting. The third level is called independent application, the ability to practice the new competency back in the workplace without the relative safety of being in a learning environment. Finally, the highest level of mastery is skilled performance, which requires fully integrating the new competency into one's skill set to the point that an individual can perform it almost without thinking. (See figure 5.1 for a graphical representation of this concept.) With each successive step, the required development time, effort, and intensity are increased. Hence, moving leaders to a mastery level of critical awareness and knowledge requires less time and intensity than moving them to a level of guided application, and so on.

In our experience, a powerful leadership development experience will result in a variety of levels of mastery. The reason is that in any role, there are some areas of competency that are critical for effective performance of one's job and others that are secondary. Utilizing a levels-of-mastery framework for prioritization of the competencies enables groups to acknowledge the full breadth of competencies required for performance yet supports them in determining which competencies to focus more time and effort on.

The levels-of-mastery model is based loosely on the concept of a hierarchy of learning that addressed cognitive, affective, and psychomotor development levels (Bloom, Mesia, & Krathwohl, 1964a, 1964b). Although similar in noting that different types of experiences are required to accomplish different types of learning, the levels-of-mastery model is unique. It focuses on levels of performance and is used to guide decision making related to designing leadership development curricula. By knowing which competencies are to be developed to critical awareness and knowledge, guided application, independent application, and skilled performance, designers know which competencies need only information dissemination (including the receipt and debriefing of 360-degree feedback), which need practice experiences in the context of the program itself, which should be the focus of short-term coaching and practice in the workplace, and which require more extensive coaching and practice.

In the case of the middle managers of the CIA, three of the thirty-three competencies were identified as needing significant development resources to reach the skilled performance level of mastery, nineteen were identified as requiring post-program coaching and practice efforts to reach the independent application level, eight required only practice experiences within the context of the program itself, and three required only information dissemination.

Conceptualizing the Delivery Framework

The sixth step of the LDIA involves putting it all together to form a draft design for the initiative. This exercise enables the design team to map out how delivery of the initiative will flow over time. The design at this phase is very rough. For example, it would show the points at which face-to-face training, coaching, assessment and feedback, practice activities, and other components are to take place in relation to each other. In this way, the design

Figure 5.1. Levels-of-Mastery Framework

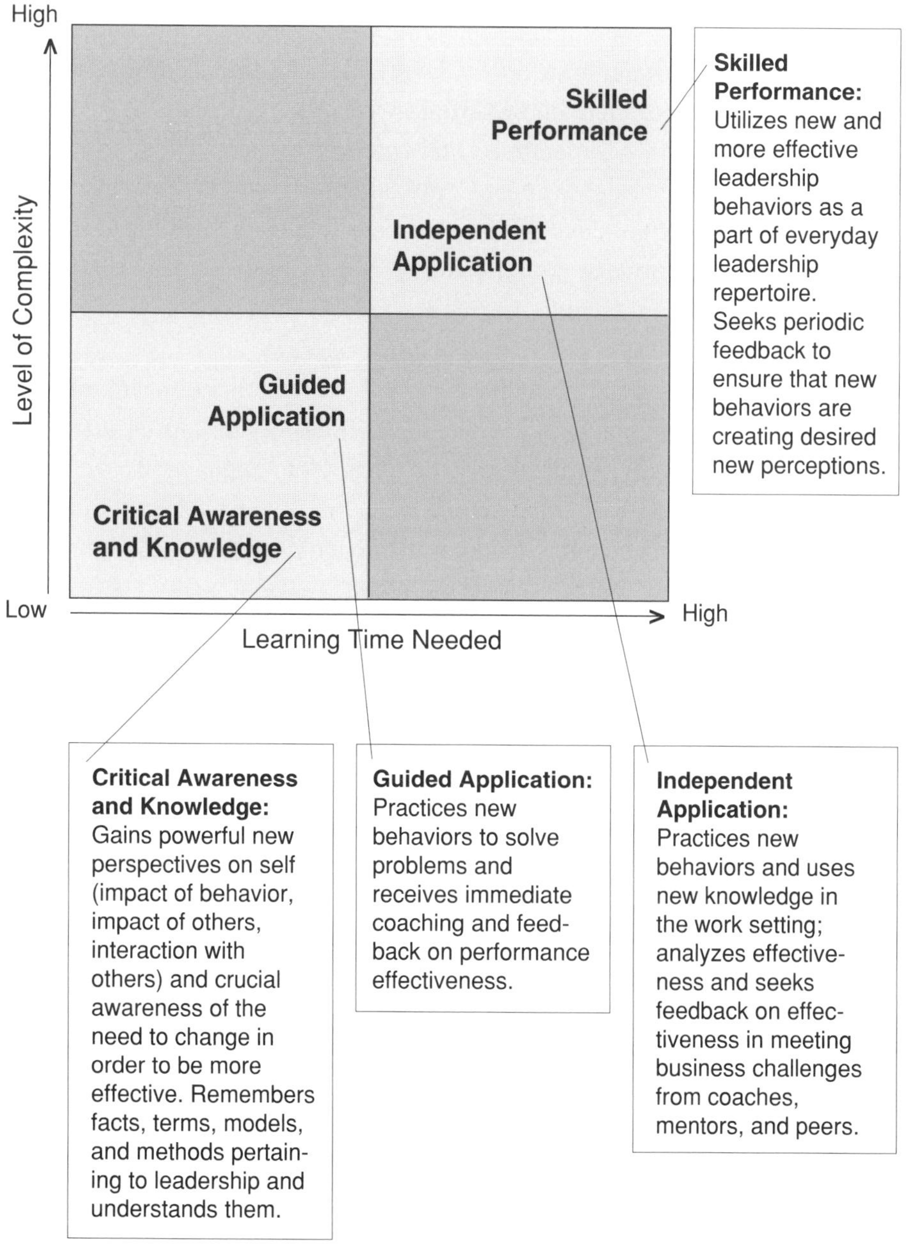

High

Level of Complexity

Low

Skilled Performance

Independent Application

Guided Application

Critical Awareness and Knowledge

Learning Time Needed

High

Skilled Performance: Utilizes new and more effective leadership behaviors as a part of everyday leadership repertoire. Seeks periodic feedback to ensure that new behaviors are creating desired new perceptions.

Critical Awareness and Knowledge: Gains powerful new perspectives on self (impact of behavior, impact of others, interaction with others) and crucial awareness of the need to change in order to be more effective. Remembers facts, terms, models, and methods pertaining to leadership and understands them.

Guided Application: Practices new behaviors to solve problems and receives immediate coaching and feedback on performance effectiveness.

Independent Application: Practices new behaviors and uses new knowledge in the work setting; analyzes effectiveness and seeks feedback on effectiveness in meeting business challenges from coaches, mentors, and peers.

team is able to create a design that is acceptable to their organizational culture and based on the leadership competencies to be developed at the level of mastery desired for each competency. This step concludes with a concept "drawing"—a framework—of the entire initiative.

For example, the framework shown in figure 5.2 was designed for the CIA's middle management level, where the competencies found under the Middle Manager heading in exhibit 5.2 were identified as needing to be developed to their associated levels of mastery.

The value of the competencies and levels of mastery at this point is that together they enable design teams to truly understand the relationship between what they want to develop, how it needs to be developed, and the resulting resource implications. In the case shown above, experiential activities were designed to take place during the face-to-face session to move participants to a guided application level of mastery on specific competencies. The coaching sessions following the face-to-face session are meant to guide participants to an independent practice level of mastery on those same competencies. Hence, the competencies provide a common language that helps the design team in talking with others about the design (at subsequently increasing levels of detail). And competencies enable the design of evaluation methods because they indicate the types of changes (that is, outcomes) expected.

Conceptualizing the Evaluation Process

The final step results in an evaluation plan. In short, the LDIA is a structured process that targets leadership development to organizational-level outcomes, using logic to connect the various parts. This last step defines the outcomes by enabling the design team to determine the kinds of evidence stakeholders will accept as proof of program impact and the types of data needing to be gathered. The focus group answers questions such as the following: Do our stakeholders want normative group assessment profiles showing how our leaders compare to leaders in similar industries? Do they want survey results showing how coworkers see the participants behaving differently as leaders six months after the program? Do they want measures that illustrate the organization has benefited in a specific way as a result of leadership development? As a result, the evaluation design will connect the leadership development initiative and its intended outcomes to the organizational and leadership challenges identified in earlier steps in a way that leads both the initiative itself and the evaluation to form a strategic approach to meeting organizational needs. The role of the evaluation is in identifying

Figure 5.2. Draft Design for Middle Managers' Program

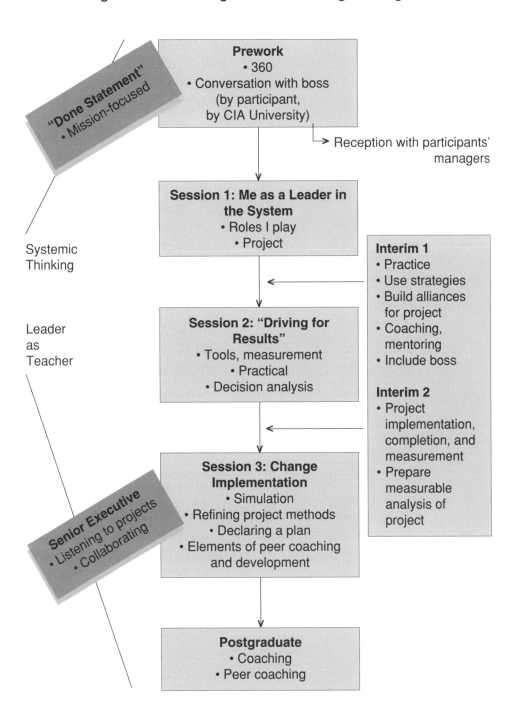

whether the outcomes were met and to what extent; what additional development may be needed for the target group; how the organization itself contrib-
uted to the success or failure of the initiative (in the form of facilitating
factors such as boss support for development or barriers such as lack of a
connection between the leadership development initiative and performance
evaluation systems); and whether, how, and how quickly the initiative needs
to be redesigned.

The Design Team

One of the key success factors for the CIA's needs assessment and conceptual
design process was that the same core team of organization members and
associates was consistent throughout the LDIA implementation for the supervisor, manager, and executive initiatives. At the same time, there also was
considerable fluidity in the participant audience across the three different
LDIAs (one for each level of management) that was intentional, allowing the
best-informed group of people to be present at the appropriate sessions. The
benefit of including different sets of experts for each LDIA was in bringing
the perspective of the target population of leaders to the process, infusing
each LDIA with subject matter expertise for the given population of
managers. The successful implementation of a model with a core team plus
population-specific subject matter experts assumes that design decisions are
more effective and applicable when multiple participants come to a collective
decision about what values and competencies are most important in an
organization.

    At the same time, forming a large working group that has representa-
tives from all critical stakeholders—for instance, the target population, their
managers, HR, consultants working with the target population, and so on—
results in a large, unwieldy group that is slow to move and make decisions. A
strong design team will have the core team that is ultimately responsible for,
and accountable for, the design and development of the program yet has made
an agreement with the other team members that their input will be taken
seriously. The design team must be open to hearing and utilizing input that
they don't necessarily agree with, especially when that input is coming from
people close to the target population. It is tempting to say that this creates
buy-in. But the principle is more basic and sincere: it is about getting the best
information in an efficient process so that the final product makes sense and
is of obvious relevance, thus serving the intended population effectively.

Content of the Models

During the first step of the LDIA, the organizational challenges facing the CIA as a whole were not unlike those faced by managers at all levels in other organizations.

Organizational Challenges

Overcome bureaucracy. The processes and regulations put in place over the years to govern activities are often an impediment to the effective performance of the organization's mission in an era when agility and flexibility are paramount. This is a challenge faced by many large organizations, regardless of the sector they represent (Hogan, 2005).

Break down stovepipes. The necessary differentiation of tasks in the organization over fifty-seven years had led to the creation of stovepipes, or functional silos, that stifle the exchange of vital information between parts of the organization and with other organizations. In an era when rapid information exchange is vital to national and global security, these stovepipes must be broken down. We often hear this challenge vocalized by clients in the corporate sector, as well, who have had growth that led to a lack of communication and collaboration across divisions or departments (Ashkenas, Ulrich, Jick, & Kerr, 1995).

Increase speed and agility. In an era when terrorist incidents and war are part of our daily news and when communication can be instantaneous, the need for speed and agility in handling, analyzing, and responding to incoming intelligence is vital to national security. While few companies face the threat of terrorism on a daily basis, speed and agility are issues for many types of organizations in which markets, economies, and technologies can literally change overnight (Hamel & Prahalad, 1994).

Manage growth, recruitment, and retention. Because much of the expertise to do intelligence work can only be developed once a person is working for the organization, recruiting the right people and then retaining them are absolutely vital. As is not the case in many other types of organizations, firing an employee with secret or top secret clearance from the CIA has serious implications for national and global security. It is very important for this organization to bring the right people on board and develop them throughout their careers. In a world with an ever more shallow talent pool, attraction, selection, and retention have become paramount (Chambers, Foulon, Handfield-Jones, Hankin, & Michaels, 1998).

Manage multiple critical priorities. Because the nature of the threat to national security has changed from one that required a fairly narrow focus in the cold war to multiple and more amorphous threats in the war on terror, managers must be able to balance numerous critical priorities. In many ways, this is no different from the challenges faced by other types of organizations with conflicting pressures and competing values (Quinn, 1988).

Balance tactical and strategic focus. Because 9/11 created such an urgency to focus on the prevention of further terrorist incidents, CIA managers have been pushed toward a much more tactical focus on "what's now." This has taken away from thinking about "what's coming." Ultimately this does not serve the nation well. Managers need the tools to be able to balance the two. Many leaders in other sectors face the same pressures of time that limit the extent to which they are able to think strategically about the future while consistently hitting short-term targets (Kaplan & Kaiser, 2003).

Improve trust and empowerment. Managers cannot do it all. Employees must work in an environment that encourages initiative and risk. To do so requires that managers learn to create a high-trust environment in which managers can let go of control and employees and managers can trust each other. Although decisions may have life-or-death consequences for the CIA, nearly all organizations in the modern world strive to push decision making down and be more participative while also retaining speed and accountability (Vroom & Jago, 1988).

Leadership Needs, Competencies, and Levels of Mastery

The LDIA process was specifically constructed to provide structure to what can be, at times, a loose process that results in a flimsy model overloaded with concessions made to several stakeholders. The risk is a lack of focus that won't provide the guidance needed for leadership development purposes. It is important to recognize that this particular process is not intended to produce a competency model that will hold up to the validation required for selection competency models. A selection competency model must be developed with much greater rigor and will, therefore, take more than two days to develop. Hence, we actually do not call what the LDIA process produces a competency model at all—we know the difference and don't want our clients to misunderstand what they are getting. For leadership development purposes, however, this process results in a set of competencies that has face validity and is far more valid in other ways (with regard to leadership development needs) than many organizations are accustomed to having.

Through the next three steps, the LDIA process resulted in thirty-three competencies that needed to be developed for supervisors, thirty-three for middle managers, and eighteen for executives. These are listed in exhibit 5.2. The competencies for each population of managers are also broken out by levels of mastery. The competencies shown in the top row of the table were those to be developed to a level of critical awareness and knowledge or guided application. This means that either participants needed to be made fundamentally aware of the importance of a particular competency and of their relative strength or development need in that area (critical awareness and knowledge), or they also needed to be given opportunities to practice new approaches to that competency in the safety of the facilitated training environment (guided application). Competencies shown in the middle row of the table indicate that the development process needed to be designed to encourage participants to practice a new competency in the workplace until they were able to use it with relative comfort (independent application). Finally, competencies shown in the bottom row indicate that some degree of facilitated process, such as coaching, needed to be included in the design of the program to ensure that participants were able to practice the new competency in the workplace to the extent of becoming very comfortable with their performance in that area (skilled performance).

Similarities across Levels

Comparing the critical competencies across the three levels, there are six competencies shared by them all: influence, leadership, and power; acting systemically; change management; learning from mistakes; integrity; and ethics/culture. These are consistent with an organization whose challenges involve making a change from operating within different silos to operating as an integrated organization, while at the same time maintaining the ethics and integrity required in the type of work they do. Learning from mistakes rather than repeating mistakes is another crucial competency for people at all levels, for in today's CIA, mistakes can result in inefficiencies at the least and national tragedy at the extreme. All levels are required to understand their roles in influencing others through leadership and responsible power. Highlighting these six competencies at all three levels emphasizes their importance to participants in leadership development as they make their way through the pipeline of leadership responsibility. Thus, these competencies become a core

Exhibit 5.2. Competency Models for Three Levels of Management in the CIA

Levels of Mastery	Organizational Levels		
	Supervisor	Middle Manager	Executive
Critical Awareness and Knowledge, Guided Application	Relationships Compassion and sensitivity Leveraging differences Influence, leadership, and power Doing whatever it takes Change management Openness to influence and flexibility Handling disequilibrium Self-awareness Self-management, insight Learning from mistakes Integrity	Relationships Compassion and sensitivity Confronting problem employees Resourcefulness Embracing flexibility Handling disequilibrium Adapting to cultural differences Having the courage to take risks Openness to influence and flexibility Seeking opportunities to learn Learning from mistakes	Putting people at ease Relationship building Influence, leadership, and power Taking action, making decisions, following through Leadership stature Resourcefulness Change management Acting systemically Risk taking and innovation Having the courage to take risks Learning from mistakes Ethics, culture Acting with integrity Integrity Customer support and relations
Independent Application	Relationship building Bringing out the best in others Motivating others Delegating Selecting, developing, and accepting people	Employee development Bringing out the best in others Motivating others Delegating Selecting, developing, and accepting people	

Exhibit 5.2. Competency Models for Three Levels of Management in the CIA (cont.)

	Organizational Levels		
Levels of Mastery	Supervisor	Middle Manager	Executive
Independent Application (cont.)	Organizing Planning and goal setting Problem solving, decision making Acting systemically Taking action, making decisions, and following through Communication Listening Getting information, making sense of it Seeking and using feedback Giving feedback Managing conflict Confronting problem employees Ethics, culture	Participative management Listening Leading people Influence, leadership, and power Decisiveness Change management Acting systemically Getting information, making sense of it Seeking broad business knowledge Seeking and using feedback Managing conflict Acting with integrity Integrity Ethics, culture	Vision Planning and goal setting
Skilled Performance	Employee development Seeking opportunities to learn Customer and vendor relations	Vision Leadership stature Administrative, organizational ability	Self-awareness

that threads through the entire developmental process. At any given point in time, the chain of hierarchy within any particular department will be exposed to these competencies in a way that creates a common language and culture around them, creating consistency in what supervisors and their managers, for example, learn is important for success.

Other similarities in the competencies identified at different levels are highlighted in exhibit 5.3. Here, each of the three levels of management is compared with the other two, one pair at a time.

Differences across Levels

We now turn our attention to what is unique about the competency models for the three levels. What is interesting about comparing the three competency models in exhibit 5.2 is how the level of mastery required for competencies changes across the three levels. For example, whereas all three levels will experience development targeting the area of change management, the specific means and intensity of development will vary because supervisors need to achieve critical awareness and knowledge, middle managers need to master independent practice, and executives need to master guided application. In this particular case, the middle managers are the change agents; it is at this level that significant changes will be initiated, which is commonly the case in a large, multilayered organization (Huy, 2002). The executives will set strategy regarding some aspect of the Agency that needs to be changed. The middle managers are then responsible for determining how, exactly, the change can be made. They will identify the processes and procedures that need to be changed, and how. Upon initiating the change, they are responsible for allocating resources and helping supervisors understand the changes and how to implement them. They must influence the supervisors to support and execute the changes. The supervisors, then, need to have an awareness of the issues related to change management, but their main role of implementing the changes as determined by their middle managers means that the supervisors are not responsible for key decisions about what will change and how it will be accomplished.

Some other differences across levels are seen in the competencies selected for only one level. For example, the supervisory role is the first level at which leaders in the CIA have responsibility for other employees—the first time in the movement up the ladder when they are not solely individual contributors. Therefore, these leaders must be able to solve problems and

---

Exhibit 5.3. Critical Competencies Common to Different Levels of Managers

Supervisors and Middle Managers	Middle Managers and Executives	Supervisors and Executives
Relationships	Vision	Self-awareness
Compassion, sensitivity	Leadership stature	Relationship building
Listening	Having the courage to take risks	Planning and goal setting
Selecting, developing, and accepting people	Resourcefulness	Taking action, making decisions, and following through
Bringing out the best in others	Acting with integrity	
Employee develop-ment		
Motivating others		
Delegating		
Seeking opportunities to learn		
Seeking and using feedback		
Getting information, making sense of it		
Handling disequilibrium		
Openness to influence and flexibility		
Managing conflict		

---

make decisions that are accepted by their direct reports. This includes decisions that are likely to be unpopular; thus supervisors need the savvy to help their staffs understand and accept the rationale for these tough calls and then model ways for dealing with them.

Middle managers typically have five to seven years of supervisory experience and play the key integrating role between the executive management chains (which possess the monetary resources) and the supervisors who are overseeing the work, enabling the latter to "get the product out the door," so to speak. The competencies that are developed at this level and not others include participative management, decisiveness, seeking broad business knowledge, and administrative and organizational ability. This reflects the unique challenges of what the CIA Leadership Academy calls "managing and leading change from the middle"—being responsible and responsive to both the level above and the level below in a way that is qualitatively different from the "middle place" experienced by supervisors. The responsibilities of the middle managers necessitate that they move away from hands-on involvement in doing "the work" (that is, the product) themselves in any way and learn how to work in a way that supports others in doing so, while at the same time playing a role in interpreting changes determined from executives above and framing the implications of those changes for employees in their part of the organization.

The competencies noted solely for executives include customer support and relations, putting people at ease, and risk taking and innovation. These competencies, together, reflect the needs of a level that usually has more public exposure; executives must carry themselves in a way that reflects the confidence and calm of the organization in sometimes trying times. And they must break out of traditional mind-sets to identify innovative solutions to organizational challenges.

The Resulting Programs

Reflecting the similarities and differences shown above, the resulting development experiences for cultivating each competency set to the given level of mastery are both similar and different. The differences reflect customization and respect for the unique challenges facing each of the three levels. The similarities result in intentional overlap that does not require participants to "repeat" the same content or experience but to build on the learning at one level as they proceed to the next. This is beneficial because the likelihood that individuals would participate in all three development initiatives during their tenure at the organization is high. However, when appropriate, the designs reuse specific aspects of content or experience to enable participants to develop awareness and skill from the perspectives of their current levels of responsibility and accountability.

The programs for each of the three levels take place over several months. The programs include a combination of traditional, face-to-face training sessions with a variety of delivery mechanisms, such as presentation of content, opportunities for practice (in the form of short and multiday simulations), assessment and feedback regarding participants' baseline performance levels on many of the competencies before attending the program, periods of one-on-one and peer-coaching interventions, and some type of work-based project or assignment that serves as a real-world practice activity for helping participants transfer their learning back to the workplace.

To provide an example of the intentional design features used, we will use the remaining space to highlight the relationship between the supervisors' and middle managers' programs.

Data Collection

The supervisor and middle manager programs (as well as the executive program) use online brainstorming techniques to examine issues, challenges, and values pertinent to participants at that moment in time. These data are threaded throughout the program as shared and understood linkages between the training and development experience and the real-time demands back on the job. In addition, the data from the most recent runs of each program are shared with the other programs (that is, for the other levels), creating a shared understanding of the similarities and differences in the nature of the pressing business issues across the three levels of management.

Emphasis on Conflict

In the supervisors' program, participants use a self-scoring assessment of their conflict management style combined with a content delivery module on the same topic. In the middle managers' program, participants use the 360-degree version of the same assessment and work on an unresolved conflict in their units during the program. Hence, they are building awareness of conflict issues during the supervisors' program and are getting feedback from others and addressing real conflict as part of the middle managers' program. If individuals were to transition from the supervisory to the managerial level and participate in both programs during their tenure, the awareness created during the supervisory program would enable middle managers to transition into acceptance of feedback and real-world application of that learning regarding conflict more readily.

Outcome Focus

All of the programs have a definitive focus on outcomes. As indicated by the levels of mastery identified for each of the competencies, the intent of these programs is to make a change in the behavior and performance of the participants to the extent that there is a notable impact at the organizational level that results from these changes. "Driving for results" addresses a set of outcome-related competencies in both the supervisors' and middle managers' program. Two days are devoted to this topic in the supervisory program, and three days in the middle managers' program. Also in the middle managers' program, the topic is continuously tied back to a job challenge each participant works on during the entire multipart program.

Focus on Feedback

The ability to give feedback to others is addressed in both programs in very different ways. Giving feedback relates to several competencies, such as listening and developing employees. During the supervisors' program, situational leadership theory (Hersey & Blanchard, 1969) is used as a starting place to help supervisors learn how to give feedback to their employees. The middle managers are introduced to giving feedback, but to avoid repeating previous content, those who were exposed to it through the supervisory program are referred to a special-topics course on feedback for more information and skill building.

Focus on Change

Supervisors are exposed to change management from the perspective of their role as implementers of change identified by their middle managers. The middle managers' program, in contrast, is designed in such a way that the entire focus is on initiating change by translating strategic direction into clear goals, devising an operating plan for achieving them, and helping supervisors execute the changes. Both programs use the same self-assessment on preferences for change. The type of change competencies needed play out differently at the two levels. For example, change implementers need to enlist people in change, while the change initiators must frame and communicate the change agenda, build alliances, and map out operating plans. In this way, it is clear how the two roles require different networks of collaboration.

Similarity in Assessment

Both programs make use of the same general 360-degree feedback assessment of leadership performance. However, the content of that assessment is different across the three levels, reflecting the unique models presented in exhibit 5.2. Each program is designed to extend application and impact beyond the program itself through the use of learning opportunities as well as opportunities for consultation and coaching by others toward a particular issue one is facing. Ongoing assessment is a key component to monitoring impact and progress.

Conclusion

In this chapter, we attempt to illustrate the use of competency models across three levels of hierarchy in an organization to create a common leadership development platform that is connected in some ways across each level yet enables each level to have its own identifiable features designed specifically for that level's needs. The outcome of the process used by the CIA to identify the needs of leaders at the three levels resulted in three different sets of competencies that overlapped in some ways and not in others. Hence, the resulting programs reflected a similar blend of customized integration.

The use of competency models for leadership development purposes is not really new, but the focus of an organization on the competencies that might be required for success within its realm versus some general model of leadership competency is a relatively new twist in the field of leadership development. Certainly, identifying competencies specifically for purposes of creating a leadership development initiative (versus a model that exists for many personnel-related reasons, such as selection, promotion, and development) has crept into the field in the last decade. It has emerged as organizations have shifted their efforts from using leadership development for general developmental purposes and as rites of passage as leaders moved into specific levels in the hierarchy to using leadership development for purposes of accomplishing strategic outcomes. In that way, strategic direction and institutional purpose are the driving forces that define the needs and curriculum design for leader development, ensuring relevance and optimizing impact.

Certainly, there are many ways in which organizations and leadership development providers identify competencies to be the focus of leadership development efforts. It is our hope that the method we describe here provides some ideas for how to efficiently create competency models that have both the requisite variety needed to serve unique populations as well as a foundation of similarity that integrates leader development across the organization. This method, its results, and the resulting program designs are meeting the needs of the CIA Leadership Academy. This approach has proven helpful in producing highly effective leaders throughout three levels of the organization. In that way, leadership development has become a vehicle for leading the organization through substantial and urgent changes. Its success in meeting this challenge will be measured by the CIA's effectiveness in preserving the national security of the United States in a world forever changed in the last few years.

Note

The 360 by Design instrument is a trademark of the Center for Creative Leadership.

References

Ashkenas, R., Ulrich, D., Jick, T., & Kerr, S. (1995). *The boundaryless organization: Breaking the chains of organizational structure.* San Francisco: Jossey-Bass.

Bloom, B. S., Mesia, B. B., & Krathwohl, D. R. (1964a). *Taxonomy of educational objectives: Vol. 1. The affective domain.* New York: David McKay.

Bloom, B. S., Mesia, B. B., & Krathwohl, D. R. (1964b). *Taxonomy of educational objectives: Vol. 2. The cognitive domain.* New York: David McKay.

Chambers, E. G., Foulon, M., Handfield-Jones, H., Hankin, S. M., & Michaels, E. G., III. (1998). The war for talent. *The McKinsey Quarterly, 3,* 44–57.

Hamel, G., & Prahalad, C. K. (1994). *Competing for the future.* Boston: Harvard Business School Press.

Hersey, P., & Blanchard, K. (1969). Life cycle theory of leadership. *Training and Development Journal, 2,* 6–34.

Hogan, R. T. (2005, April). The secret life of organizations. In R. B. Kaiser (Chair), *Making leadership research more relevant.* Symposium presented at the Twentieth Annual Conference of the Society for Industrial and Organizational Psychology, Los Angeles.

Huy, Q. (2002). Emotional balancing: The role of middle managers in radical change. *Administrative Science Quarterly, 47,* 31–36.

Kaplan, R. E., & Kaiser, R. B. (2003). Developing versatile leadership. *MIT Sloan Management Review, 44*(4), 19–26.

Lombardo, M. M., & Eichinger, R. W. (2002). *The leadership machine.* Minneapolis, MN: Lominger Limited.

Quinn, R. E. (1988). *Beyond rational management.* San Francisco: Jossey-Bass.

Sessa, V. I., Kaiser, R., Taylor, J. K., & Campbell, R. J. (1998). *Executive selection: A research report on what works and what doesn't.* Greensboro, NC: Center for Creative Leadership.

Vroom, V. H., & Jago, A. G. (1988). *The new leadership: Managing participation in organizations.* Englewood Cliffs, NJ: Prentice Hall.